Åke Hultkrantz / Ørnulf Vorren (Ed.)

THE HUNTERS

heir Culture and Way of Life

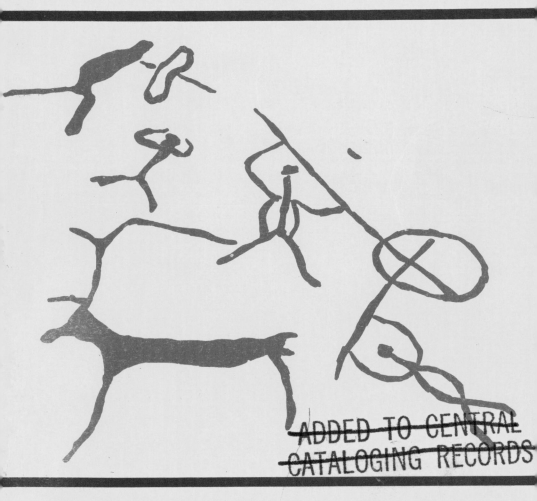

Universitetsforlaget

THE HUNTERS

THE HUNTERS

Their Culture and Way of Life

Edited by Åke Hultkrantz and Ørnulf Vorren

Tromsø Museum Skrifter VOL. XVIII

Universitetsforlaget
Tromsø – Oslo – Bergen

© Universitetsforlaget 1982
ISBN 82-00-05910-3
Cover design: Stig Helge Hansen

Printed in Norway
by Edgar Høgfeldt A.s - Kristiansand S.

Preface

During the past fifteen years anthropological research, in the widest sense of this term, has focused an increasing interest on the cultural forms and life-ways of the hunters. Scholars with different research specialities have concerned themselves with diverse aspects of the hunting culture. Once this culture embraced the whole of mankind, and it did so for many hundred thousands of years. Reminiscences of this old culture continue among us to this very day. They occur in surviving marginal cultures, and in a more or less modified form they emerge in hunting traditions and other conservative fields of today's western culture.

It is therefore not surprising that several recent works deal with the culture of the hunters in wider perspectives. Interdisciplinary symposia have been arranged to meet the demands of cross-cultural comparisons. In particular we should mention here the large symposium on *Man the Hunter* that was held at the University of Chicago in April, 1966. It was organized by Sol Tax, Richard B. Lee, and Irven DeVore, and sponsored by the Wenner-Gren Foundation for Anthropological Research. The papers of the symposium were printed in 1968, edited by Lee and DeVore under the afore-mentioned title (Chicago: Aldine Publishing Company). The assembled students at the Chicago meeting, about seventy-five from different countries, concentrated their discussions on topics that have recently been considered urgent and important in the USA. Questions of ecology, economics, social organization, demography, and evolution dominated the debate. Such essential aspects of hunting culture as material culture, technology, art and religion were omitted. The enormous scope of the subject made such a limitation perfectly natural.

There is no doubt that the themes chosen by the Chicago symposium are very basic indeed for our understanding of hunting cultures. Nevertheless, from a Northern European point of view it is just as important that those aspects of hunting culture that have been particularly studied in our part of the world — material culture, technology, and religion — should be objects of detailed investigations. Ecological conditions and historical traditions have, in combination or interaction, created the prerequisites of the cultural potentials and the spiritual deportment that convey to the hunting culture its profile. In material culture, technology, and religion, these cultural processes obtain their adequate expression.

At the instigation of Åke Hultkrantz and Johannes Nicolaisen, the Nordic Council of Anthropological Research decided to arrange a symposium on *The Culture and Way of Life of the Hunters* in Tromsø, Norway, in 1979. The Council is a cross-disciplinary organization of researchers in Northern Europe (Denmark, Finland, Iceland, Norway and Sweden) that serves both as a research assembly and a trade union. It has arranged several symposia in the past (for instance, on *Circumpolar Problems* in 1969). Since in these countries anthropology is not a united discipline as it is in Anglo-Saxon countries, various representatives of disciplines that may be called anthropological have taken part in the symposia (together with distinguished guests from other countries). At the 1979 symposium on hunters, all the participants were from the Nordic countries, except one who was from Canada. They represented an array of subjects: archaeology, history, ethnology, ethnography, social anthropology, linguistics, folklore and comparative religion.

The symposium was located in Tromsø, since there are, in the surroundings of this attractive town in beautiful northern Norway, a good many remains of pre-historic and historic hunting culture: corrals, systems of pitfalls, sacrificial enclosures, stone idols, rock drawings. Most of these remains stem from the Saamis (Lapps). The symposium became a mobile conference with incessant excursions into the mountains and down to the fiord valleys and remote coastal islands. These activities corresponded to particular sections of the lecture program, an ideal arrangement which – unfortunately – cannot be shared by the readers. Ørnulv Vorren and Povl Simonsen were the organizers and expert guides of the Tromsø symposium. Economic subsidies from the Nordic Cultural Foundation (*Nordisk Kulturfond*) and the University of Tromsø which were generously put at the disposal of the organizing committee made the symposium possible.

It is natural that the Tromsø symposium cannot be compared to the gigantic Chicago symposium with its world-wide selection of contributors and its enormous economic resources. Still, it was in a way a complement to this symposium, its papers illuminating, as has been said, important aspects that the Chicago symposium did not deal with. It is, we hope, understandable that scholars from the Nordic countries could not provide a full series of presentations of hunting cultures, or covering accounts of material culture, technology, art and religion within such cultures. Owing to the small number of Nordic scholars who study hunters, the selection of papers presented in this book will prove very uneven. Only selected aspects of the rich and varied cultures of the hunters can be presented. Some important items, like housing, clothing, rites of passage and shamanism are not represented here, except casually. Nor are there any papers on social organization and other topics that were dealt with in *Man the Hunter*. In particular the editors deplore the lack of contributions on tropical and sub-tropical hunters. Professor Nicolaisen should have written these sections, but his illness and death prevented the book from becoming rounded off in this respect. As it stands, the volume has a heavy Arctic and sub-Arctic slant. Perhaps this is not so bad after all: it reflects the state of research in the Nordic countries.

It remains for the editors to thank the money-raising organizations – the Nordic Cultural Foundation, and the University of Tromsø – for their magnanimous aid.

The book has been dedicated to the memory of Johannes Nicolaisen, a fine scholar, valued colleague, and great friend.

Åke Hultkrantz   *Ørnulv Vorren*

Contents

Introduction
The Culture of the Hunters
– Man's Oldest Culture

Åke Hultkrantz

Anthropologists – and here I mean representatives of many disciplines that may be referred to as anthropological – have during the last decade increasingly paid attention to the pre-human roots of human behaviour. Students of ethology, biogram research, and socio-biology (or bio-social anthropology) have been able to reveal deep ties between animals and man. Present-day behaviour in human societies may, perhaps, be linked with and explained by the behaviour of animals.[1]

Such a perspective gives a new meaning to the studies of hunting cultures. During the incomparably greatest part of its history humankind has been composed of hunters and gatherers. Agriculture, pastoral nomadism, and urbanism did not appear on the scene until very recently – agriculture 10–15000 years ago, urbanism some 5000 years ago. All the preceding time our ancestors and other human beings were hunters, fishermen and collectors. William Laughlin, pointing out the important fact that man practised hunting for 99 per cent of his history, writes:

Hunting is the master behavior pattern of the human species. It is the organizing activity which integrated the morphological, physiological, genetic, and intellectual aspects of the individual human organisms and of the population who compose our single species. Hunting is a way of life, not simply a 'subsistence technique', which importantly involves commitments, correlates, and consequences spanning the entire biobehavioral continuum of the indivdual and of the entire species of which he is a member (Laughlin 1968: 304).

Similarly, David Hamburg concludes that much of our genetic equipment was probably shaped by the selective pressures of the long hunting era. He also suggests that 'some of the values that were useful in solving adaptive problems during the hunting and gathering era may still persist in the face of very recent environmental changes' (Hamburg 1968: 339).

11

In other words, during the hunting age we humans were formed, biologically and mentally, for our cultural evolution. We were 'programmed' for a way of behaviour that still persists. At that early date there originated the first instruments to satisfy our cultural requirements, the first technological achievements, the first social organization, the first artistic idea, the first religious responses. In a wider evolutionary perspective all later human activity is a successive continuation of these beginnings.

It is considerations of this kind that reveal why research on the hunters and their way of life is so extremely important.

New research in palaeoanthropology suggests that the origins of culture antedate humanization. The use of implements and formation of social groups may already be discerned among our next of kin neighbours, the apes. Investigations of chimpanzee ethology have reduced the gap between man and the animals. The physical evolution from apelike primate to man has been illuminated in a revolutionary way through the recent discoveries of hominids of considerable age. I refer here in particular to the skeleton finds made along the Rift Valley in East Africa, among them the remains of *Homo habilis* in Olduvai Gorge, unearthed by the Leakey family. Here was a hominid with an expanded brain who was evidently using tools.[2]

In the early summer of 1978 I was privileged to take part in the international Nobel symposium on Current Argument on Early Man, which the Royal Swedish Academy of Sciences arranged in Karlskoga, Sweden (Königsson 1980). It is rewarding to study the results of this symposium as well as some other contemporary writings by one of the participants in the symposium (Isaac 1978), since they have a bearing on the problem of the oldest evidence of human hunting culture. Some of the information used in the following derives from the discussion at the symposium and has not been printed. I want to stress one point in this connection, however. The leading scholars of the symposium all agreed that there was no consensus in their field. The reconstruction of possible lines of development that follows here is not universally accepted, but presents interpretations of the evidence that have been launched and have appealed to the present writer.

If we scrutinize the African evidence we shall find that, as Phillip V. Tobias states, the date of about 2.5 million years B.P. constituted a divide in the evolution of hominids. From then on, a plurality of heterogeneous forms takes place. More important still for us, stone and bone objects from this time suggest that from now on it is the mechanisms of culture rather than hominid evolution that determine the course of development (David Pilbeam).

Most interesting hunting camp sites of this early age have been disclosed by Glynn Isaac, J.W.K. Harris, and D. Crader (Isaac et al. 1976). Supported by archaeological materials from the so-called Koobi Fora Formation east of Lake Rudolf, they may have unveiled the oldest proven habitation sites we know of.[3] Unfortunately the interrelations between archaeological and fossil evidence have not been worked out, but the generalizations from the archaeological material allow certain conclusions about the contemporary condition of man.

The hominids of this area and time used implements of stone – choppers, polyhedrons, discoids, scrapers, and so on. They had produced them themselves. They were meat-eaters and made hunting expeditions to places far away from their main camps. The big game carcasses were cut up, and all the meat transported back to the home base. The transportation was facilitated by the hunters' bipedal locomotion.[4] Isaac thinks it possible to conclude there was a division of labour between the sexes, so that the men hunted while their spouses, who were more local-bound, gathered vegetables. The food was, he suggests, shared in common.

Isaac puts forward the hypothesis that these hominids had developed language capabilities and cognition (cf. Isaac 1978: 323).[5] Their spiritual life remains unknown. Maybe, as Isaac presumes, the food-sharing is a testimony of reciprocal altruism (Isaac 1978: 323) and intellectual planning (Isaac 1980: 231). One amusing detail should be mentioned here: impressions of leaves in the sediments that encase the archaeological material have led one scholar, Dr. J. Gillett, to suggest that they were leaves of a *Ficus*. Isaac and his colleagues find the reference to the role of fig leaves in the Adam and Eve myth hilarious (Isaac et al. 1976: 536). At the same they characterize their own studies as a scientific replacement 'of the Adam and Eve and other origin allegories' (Isaac et al. 1976: 550).

The archaeological discoveries in the Lake Rudolf Basin may give the oldest evidence of human (hominid) hunting culture, but to what extent does it deviate from the hunting patterns of animals? Isaac, for one, does not consider this earliest demonstrable hunting culture qualitatively different from animal hunting habits. He emphasizes that 'differences between humans and other primates are differences of degree rather than being absolute. Both meat-eating and tool-using are examples of this'. Culture, he says, is no point of difference between human and non-human

13

behavioural organizations, primarily because 'most higher mammals transmit a body of non-genetic information from generation to generation'. However, with man the volume, the complexity of this information was intensified 'by many orders of magnitude' (Isaac 1978: 313).

I do not think, however, that it is possible to link human hunting and animal foraging under the same common label. First of all, human culture is a much more qualified concept than animal culture (cf. my remarks in Moberg 1980: 18). It presupposes, moreover, man's reflections over himself, his group, and his place in existence. (The beginnings of these reflections are to my thinking the beginnings of hominization). Secondly, there is no direct hunting tradition from animals to man.

Twenty years ago Kenneth Oakley suggested that, as 'man' adapted himself to the open forest margins, he changed from being a plant and fruit eater to being in part a meat eater (Oakley 1961: 188 f.). It is quite obvious that some early hominids had to abandon the herbivorous habits of the forest apes and become carnivorous. When 14 million years ago the *Dryopithecus* gave way to the *Ramapithecus,* this change was combined with a change in habitat from forest to woodland and 'a shift in feeding behaviour, probably within the generally vegetarian complex of diets' (Pilbeam 1980: 280). C. J. Jolly has suggested that this meant seed-eating in grasslands (Jolly 1970). Some million years later, perhaps with the appearance of *Australopithecus* four to six million years ago, there was a change to open terrestrial habitat, finally resulting in incipient bipedalism and, probably, hunting. The lack of archaeological finds from so ancient times limits our knowledge of the evolution of hunting.

The general conclusion we can draw is, however, that there really was no hunting tradition to speak of from the animal stage to the hominids. Besides, animals did not create a tool-tradition that could be taken over by the emerging mankind (cf. White 1949: 40 ff.). Man, or rather his hominid predecessors, invented hunting and also the technological, material, social and ceremonial complexes surrounding hunting.

We have here so far only talked about the African progenitors of mankind. The rich variety of characters and the quantity of African hominids indicate, it seems, that man's – and the human culture's – cradle has been in Africa. The present tendency among palaeoanthropologists is to ascribe to the human genus a monocentric origin in Africa about at least 700,000 years B. P. We cannot be too sure, however. From a palaeoanthropological point of view Asia is still a *terra incognita.* Genetical investigations made by George J. Todaro suggest that man's viral gene sequence conforms to its correlative in the Asiatic apes but diverges from its correlative among the African apes. Todaro consequently argues 'a non-African origin of man millions of years ago' (Todaro 1980: 258). Scientific opinion is divided in this matter, however. We know that the so-called Java man, a *Pithecanthropus,* of whom forty fossils have been preserved, lived in Indonesia more than 1.5 million years ago. It is not known, however, whether he used artifacts (Jacob 1980).

While there is no decisive proof that man originated in Asia there is ample evidence that eastern and southern Asia has provided an early cultural development. Thus, Southeast Asia was a centre for the rise of an independent form of primitive agriculture, the cultivation of root-crops (Solheim 1972). Indeed, agriculture seems to have earlier dates here than in any other part of the world. We are reminded of Carl Sauer's speculation that agriculture as such originated in Southeast Asia (Sauer 1952). However, there is no indication that the preceding hunting culture represented a line of its own – if it now is at all possible to deduce such a fact from silent archaeological data (cf. Gorman 1971).

As it appears today, the hunting culture evolved in tropical and subtropical parts of the Old World. A very old hunting pattern, long represented in Africa and other southern regions, was later superseded by the *Steppenjägerkultur* (steppe hunting culture) that once stretched from Africa over Europe and Northern Asia to North and South America, and that may have been a result of the ecological integration of the old hunting culture with ice age conditions.

The dominant fact is however that the hunting culture, beginning at least 2.5 million years ago, more or less developed with humanization. Our life today, our thinking, our ideas of man and existence are still stamped by this circumstance.

Notes

1 I am of course fully aware that living primates do not constitute links in the evolution of man, but represent their own fulfilment, their own evolution. Experiments with chimpanzees cannot therefore enlighten human evolution other than in a most hypothetical way.
2 Research is still in its embryo, and there is a strong possibility that other places, for instance the slopes of the Himalayas, might yield evidence of the same order and quality as Olduvai Gorge (information from Richard Leakey).
3 Mary Leakey attributes to the tool-making at Olduvai Gorge an age of two million years. Before this time hominids used tools, but they did not make them.
4 Bipedalism, reduced canines, and the construction of tools have usually been re-

garded as the main proofs of humanization. However, there is no linkage in time between these traits, hominid dentitions having evolved in non-bipedal, non-tool-using creatures (Pilbeam 1980: 280 f.). Bipedalism might have originated three million years ago (Pilbeam 1980: 272).

5 Some scholars think that the development of language and culture is very late and only appeared after the human brain had reached its modern volume (Pilbeam 1980: 282). However, linguists see no possibility of explaining the absence or presence of language on the basis of anatomical factors (B. Malmberg in Moberg 1980: 18).

Bibliography

Gorman, C.
 1971 The Hoabinhian and after: Subsistence Patterns in Southeast Asia during the Late Pleistocene and Recent Periods. World Archaeology 2: 300–320.
Hamburg, D. A.
 1968 Primate Behavior and the Evolution of Aggression. Pp. 339–341 in Man the Hunter, ed. by R. B. Lee and I. DeVore. Chicago.
Isaac, G. L.
 1978 Food Sharing and Human Evolution: Archaeological Evidence from the Plio-Pleistocene of East Africa. Journal of Anthropological Research 34 (3). 311–325.
 1980 Casting the Net Wide: A Review of Archaeological Evidence for Early Hominid Land-Use and Ecological Relations. Pp. 226–251 in Königsson 1980.
Isaac, G. L., J. W. K. Harris and D. Crader
 1976 Archeological Evidence from the Koobi Fora Formation. Pp. 533–551 in Earliest Man and Environments in the Lake Rudolf Basin, ed. by Y. Coppens et al. Chicago.
Jacob, T.
 1980 The Pithecanthropus of Indonesia: Phenotype, Genetics and Ecology. Pp. 170–179 in Königsson 1980.
Jolly, C. J.
 1970 The Seed-Eaters: A New Model of Hominid Differentiation Based on a Baboon Analogy. Man 5 (1): 5–26.
Königsson, L.-K. (ed.)
 1980 Current Argument on Early Man. Oxford.
Laughlin, W. S.
 1968 Hunting: An Integrating Biobehavior System and Its Evolutionary Importance. Pp. 304–320 in Man the Hunter, ed. by R. B. Lee and I. DeVore. Chicago.
Moberg, C.-A.
 1980 Consensus, Controversy and Complications. Pp. 15–28 in Königsson 1980.
Oakley, K. P.
 1961 On Man's Use of Fire, with Comments on Tool-making and Hunting. Pp. 176–193 in Social Life of Early Man, ed. by S. L. Washburn. Viking Fund Publications in Anthropology no. 31. New York.
Pilbeam, D.
 1980 Major Trends in Human Evolution. Pp. 261–285 in Königsson 1980.

Sauer, C. O.
  1952 Agricultural Origins and Dispersals. American Geographical Society, Bowman Memorial Lectures, Series 2. New York.
Solheim, W.
  1972 An Earlier Agricultural Revolution. Scientific American 266: 34–41.
Todaro, G. J.
  1980 Evidence Using Viral Gene Sequences Suggesting An Asian Origin of Man. Pp. 252–260 in Königsson 1980.
White, L. A.
  1949 The Science of Culture. New York.

I

Hunting Techniques

Hunting is of course in the centre of attention in any hunting society. The knowledge and handiness of the hunter is of the utmost importance to his existence. Knowledge is here a double-faceted concept. It entails experience, the outcome of a long familiarity with hunting situations and the game animals. This aspect of knowledge was important in other respects too, for the most experienced hunter was very often also the headman of the hunting society. The second aspect of knowledge is learning and insight. The hunting apprentice had to be enculturated, that is, he had to learn the techniques and the rules by which the hunter could operate. Knowledge of hunting instruments and their use, of work in the task group, of social and ceremonial etiquette, of taboos and religious procedures was part of the enculturation of the young hunter.

In the following articles some parts of this knowledge are illuminated. Edvard Barth demonstrates old trapping constructions and their use in Southern Norway during prehistoric times and up to the sixteenth century. Here we are faced with old Scandinavian hunting models. In Rolf Kjellström's paper we are offered an interpretation of the enigmatic so-called Stalo sites in part of Lappland, and an analysis of Saami reindeer-hunting patterns at these sites. Ørnulv Vorren's contribution on Saami reindeer-hunting devices in the Troms area is based on his demonstrations in the field during the symposium. He shows that pitfall systems and hunting barricades are linked up with sacrificial places in an integrated hunting complex. Bo Sommarström's description of hunting methods, war patterns and rituals in Mongolia supplies evidence of the operations of the hunting tradition within the framework of a nomadic, Buddhistic society.

In this connection it should be stressed that nomadism also enters in the later phases of Saami culture (from the sixteenth century and onwards). However, the articles by Kjellström and Vorren reflect the earlier, basic hunting culture of this people.

19

Ancient Methods for Trapping Wild Reindeer in South Norway

Edvard K. Barth

Introduction

A tribe of hunting people living off game and fish survived in the forests and mountains of Scandinavia for thousands of years before the birth of Christ.

It has been ascertained that when the ice receded, the fauna made its entry about 9000 years ago, and reindeer spread over large areas in the Scandinavian mountains (Barth 1981 a). Quite soon afterwards hunters followed the deer tracks, and today the oldest known radiological datings from sites in the high mountains are from about 8500 years before the present time (Moe et. al. 1978, Bang-Andersen & Kjos-Hanssen 1979). They have been found in the Oppdal mountains south-east of Troll-heimen and in the Lærdal mountains east of the Sogne Fiord (Fig. 1). Hardangervidda, farther to the south, was covered by forest in different periods between c. 8500 to 5000 before the present (Barth et al. 1980, Barth 1981 a). Thus, variations in the climate have influenced the distribution of the reindeer during the millenia.

The distribution of the old trapping constructions and methods of hunting reindeer have been studied by the present author in central southern Norway, especially in the Rondane mountains and in Tolga and Engerdal in the northeastern part of Hedmark County, but other mountains have also been visited. All radiological data given below are calibrated ages (MASCA).

Stone-walled pitfalls with converging stone fences

With reference to available data an estimated boundary line has been drawn on a map (Fig. 1). This line indicates the area, known so far, covering finds of fully stone-walled pitfalls with converging, low stone

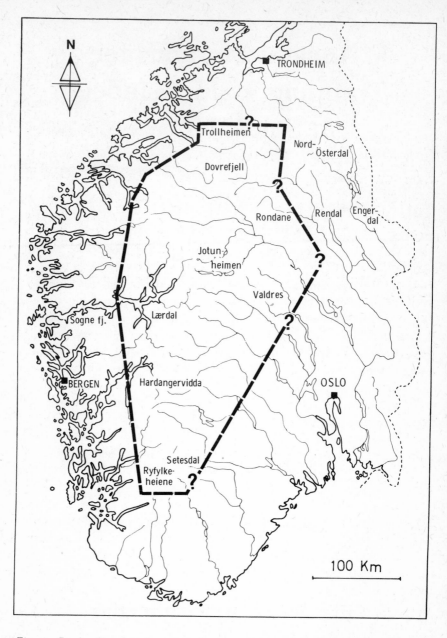

Fig. 1. Border line for the mountain area where stone-walled pitfalls have been found.

Fig. 2. Typical stone-walled pitfall with leading stone fences in the Rondane mountains.

fences leading to the four corners of the rectangular formed pit (Fig. 2). The pits were camouflaged with a vegetation layer over thin, wooden sticks (Barth 1979).

These pits are found in most areas of the mountains in the south and west, and in the north in the area from Trollheimen to North Øster-dal. In its typical form, this construction is not found east of the river Glomma in the Østerdal nor does it exist in Sweden (Barth 1975). The borderline through Valdres and southwards to Setesdal (Fig. 1) is an estimation based on different finds.

It has not been possible to trace this special kind of pitfalls in the literature from other places in Europe or in other parts of the world. There has not yet been any confirmed find of this kind in North Norway (Barth 1981).

The stone fences, about 20–50 cm high, are very typical for this kind of pitfalls. They could not lead the reindeer to the pit if the animals were frightened, as they would then certainly jump over the fences. The trapping has occurred in connection with the animal's grazing and/or walking along the ordinary animal tracks.

Øverland (1893: 243), presumably referring to Nilsson (1847: 510), tells us that a movable bar with iron points mounted on it was fastened across the pit 3/4 m way down. I very much doubt the correctness of this theory before we actually find the remains of such iron pikes in a pit. My reasoning concerns pitfalls for reindeer and moose. It is quite another matter if we refer to beasts of prey, when the preservation of the meat is not in question. Wold (1929) repeats the description of a bar with iron points, but he also mentions that sometimes a pointed pole, used for impaling the animal, should have been placed erect at the bottom of the pit.

Twice we have found the remains of a pole in stony reindeer pits indicating such an arrangement. However, in both these instances it may be correct to say that the hunters have not been able to dig as far down into the very stony bottom as was planned. In these pits we found the old bottom only 1.30 m under the ground. It is thought that they have met with solid rock or a very large stone at this depth. Therefore, it has been necessary to combine the arrangement with a pointed pole to be sure that the animal could not by force climb out of the pit.

Twice we have found the remains of another kind of pole in the pits. This pole may have lain parallel to the long axes of the pit, fastened into the walls at both ends, and quite a distance from the bottom so that the animal could only rest two feet on the bottom at the same time (the two right or the two left ones). This situation would prevent the animal from being able to jump out. We do not know how often such pitfalls were checked. If the animal was not hurt, it might live for a long time.

Probably Reusch (1897) was the first one to give both a drawing and a description from the Norwegian mountains of a stone-walled pitfall with leading stone fences. In its typical form these pits have a depth of about 2 m, a length of 2 m, and a breadth of 60–70 cm. Very few of them are now found in their original condition, but examples are found in Rondane, as shown in Fig. 3 where the pit is perfectly unchanged. The skeleton of a young reindeer at the bottom suggests that possibly in the winter wet snow in hard wind may cover the pit and then an animal may fall down. When the pits are visible, animals such as sheep never fall into them in the summer. Naturally the construction of such a pit depends on the availability of suitable stones. In Rondane this material is of the best class with particularly slaty rock, which splits into square blocks and often thin, flat slates. Very often such slates are used on edge in the walls in a pit measuring up to about 1 x 2 m in square. – It must have been a very hard job to dig out the pits in such a stony area as we find in Rondane in the whole area over 1200–1300 m altitude.

In the Rondane area so far we have registered 260 pitfalls of this

Fig. 3. One of the best preserved stone pitfalls in Rondane, 2 m deep, 1.90 m long and 0.8 m broad, and with a skeleton of a reindeer at the bottom. The slates in the short walls always stand as inverse steps.

type, most of them single, but systems of up to nine are found. Then they are always connected with long stone fences going in a continuous zigzag pattern (Fig. 4). Areas with scree often give a natural continuation of the fences. In Rondane the highest altitude for recorded pits is 1560 m a.s.l. In Jotunheimen Mølmen (1977) has a pit at an attitude of 1800 m, and K. Sveinhaug (in litt.) at 1910 m.

From 1969 to 1982 I have received 52 C14-datings of trapping constructions, of which 38 are from reindeer traps. All the dated stone-walled pits are so far from the Rondane area. The use of most of these traps stopped before the Black Death (1349).

The oldest dating so far, found in a stone-walled pit, was in the centre of Rondane 1430 m a.s.l. (Langglupdalen). The result was A.D. 40 ± 470; the great standard deviation is a consequence of the very small amount of wooden material found in this pit. The other datings of such pits are from A.D. 990 ± 50 and later. The most recent of the few datings after the Black Death is from 'A.D. 1640 or more recent'. All these datings indicate the final period of the usage of these pits. It may be very difficult to find out when such stone-walled pits came into use for the first time.

It is thought that during the Viking Age as well as the Middle Ages

25

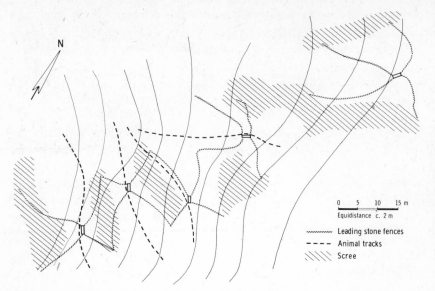

Fig. 4. Very often the leading and converging stone fences are connected with scree
areas where the animals do not like to go.

certain farms kept certain pitfalls in good condition and used them as
their own. The pits lay in the animals' ordinary grazing or migration
routes or in connection with especially rich pasture areas. When an
animal came to the camouflage layer, which gave in under the animal's
first fore-leg, it jumped forward to come clear of this suggested small
hole and then tumbled down to the bottom of the pitfall.

Øverland (1893: 243) wrote that the leading fences were up to 1–2

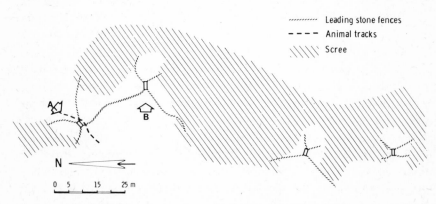

Fig. 5. Spots with grass in connection with scree may invite to the use of pitfalls
with their leading fences for passive trapping.

26

m high. This must have been taken from Nilsson (1847: 509) and cannot have been correct unless these fences were connected to a larger arrangement with an active drive of frightened animals (see below).

Fig. 5 shows an almost flat and very stony area where small grassy spots invited the animals to follow the stone fences. One of these pits was 1.65 m deep, and the earth in the bottom was wet. About 40 cm down we discovered a brownish black layer, 2 cm thick, with very small wooden fragments. Undoubtedly these were the remains of the sticks from the camouflaging layer on the top. It was dated to A.D. 1150 ± 80.

The reindeer today, as well as sheep and people, use the same animal tracks as thousands of years ago. When the trapping by pitfalls stopped a few hundred years ago, the reindeer made their way just outside the pit (see Fig. 5). Such situations can be very marked now that the Norwegian Tourist Organization has taken the old animal tracks back into use.

Earth-walled pitfalls without visible leading fences

In most of the southern Norwegian mountains we find, along the tree line, pitfalls of quite another type. They are today circular or oval shaped depressions in the earth, mostly with not a single stone visible in the walls. Plenty of wood has been available here, and undoubtedly a kind of wooden wall must have been used in the pits. Mostly this material has mouldered away and the earth walls have slipped down. Often the depressions are today about 1 m deep and at the top about 2½ x 3½ m wide (Barth 1974). Nowadays they have no visible remains of leading fences, but at the time of trapping some kind of wooden fences must have been used. These pits are often found placed along the top of moraine ridges or along the edge of gravel terraces in great numbers. In a single row there can be about one hundred pits or more, but most often they are fewer.

Such a pitfall in Rondane is shown on Fig. 6. It corresponds very much to those in the birch belt in the whole of Scandinavia. In many of the series with these pits in Rondane we sometimes find stone-walled pits and then earth pits. However, nowadays they never have marked remains of leading fences. The construction of such stone-walled pits is sometimes just the same as pitfalls in Jämtland in Sweden (Barth 1975

Fig. 6. Earth-walled pitfall in the birch wood region, today visible as a ring-formed depression.

Fig. 4). It is evident that the circular earth pitfalls along the tree line in Sweden (Selinge 1974) show a close resemblance to the Norwegian ones.

At the same time the pitfalls for moose in both Norway and Sweden have just the same appearance as for reindeer. For moose, however, the square measures at the top about 4–5 x 5–6 m (Barth 1981 b). Old judicial documents from Rendalen in Hedmark County, state that moose pitfalls were in use as late as in 1739 (Paus 1973).

Mølmen (1978) has mapped 483 pitfalls of the circular type for reindeer along the highway over Dovrefjell. Blehr (1971) points out long rows of similar kinds on the eastern part of the Hardangervidda mountain plateau.

It must have been hard work to make such long rows of pitfalls ready for use. Proudfoot (1967) has described experiments in England reproducing different activities of ancient man. A mound 12 m in diameter heaped up from material dug from a ditch 1.8 m wide and 1.2 m deep, could have been constructed in about 700 man hours when using prehistorical tools.

Middendorff 1875 (p. 1484) and 1953 (pp. 365 and 367) are the only written sources I have found concerning the use of pitfalls in Siberia among the Tungus, but nothing is said about the construction of the pits.

Burch (1972) says that pitfalls have been in use in some areas in arctic

North America, giving no details of the construction. On p. 350–365 he discusses the wild reindeer as a resource, mentioning the yearly migration in spring and autumn i Alaska and how the hunting communities utilize this situation.

In the Rondane area a marked removal southwards and northwards at certain times of the year was still observed until 12–15 years ago. Also the animal's shorter grazing routes, depending on the wind directions, result in passing several rows of pitfalls in Rondane many times during the year.

About 25 km southeast of Tolga in North Østerdal, Hedmark County, a row of about 100 pitfalls along a valley with birch wood has blocked the passage of reindeer from one mountain area to another. In one of these pits some cuts in the embankment surrounding the pit have shown a marked black layer of 1–3 cm thickness with humus and bits of charcoal. This indicates the old vegetation surface when the pit was dug out for the first time. A radiological dating resulted in 4535 ± 65 years before Christ (Barth 1979). This layer was only found in the ring-formed embankment and not in the wood around the pit.

It seems probable that a tribe of people living of hunting and fishing came to the Scandinavian peninsula very early after the glacial period. The use of pitfalls for trapping animals may have been practised in more southern parts of Europe long before this time (Barth 1981 a).

Radiological datings of remains of a wooden construction in this type of pitfall give the approximate time when the trapping with them stopped. In the central Norwegian mountains these results are placed between 155 ± 105 years before Christ and A.D. 1535 ± 95, pointing out that trapping with this kind of pitfall has been in use as long as trapping with the stone-walled ones. This parallel use could be practised in the same area with only one or two hundred metres difference in altitude (Barth 1979).

Hides for archers

It is thought that hides for hunters with bows and arrows were used several thousand years ago. It is stated that this must have been an important factor in the hunting cultures in many mountain areas in South Norway. Inside the marked area in Fig. 1 such hides are known everywhere, but occur most frequently in the Sogne Fiord and northwards and also in Engerdal to the east. They can be found as single ones or rather few, but up to about fifty in a large trapping system.

Fig. 7. The white ring shows an area with 16 hides for archers 1450 m a.s.l. at the Fremre Langhol lake in the centre of Rondane.

The occurence of such hides is always found higher than the tree line, and Mølmen (1976) has mapped shooting facilities at especially high altitudes in Jotunheimen. One of these contained 59 hides at 1900 m a.s.l. and another 9 hides at 1960 m altitude.

The hides are placed in the terrain in the same way as the pitfalls based on the hunter's experience and knowledge. The tracks and behaviour of the reindeer in relation to the wind directions must have been known in detail. Sometimes there must have been need for both the archers and other people to frighten and drive the animals in certain directions.

One of the characteristic formations in the Rondane mountains is shown in Fig. 7. Sixteen hides are found inside the white ring, situated close to the outlet of a small pond. The walls of the high mountains (more than 2000 m a.s.l.) form a 3-km long, oval area, and reindeer coming inside here enter a long, stony 'cul-de-sac'. The hunters would have driven the animals out from the bottom and towards the archers (Fig. 8). Both in this and similar situations the distance for shooting must have been very short.

The hides are always built as a stone wall, about 60–80 cm high, mostly in a half-circle formation from one to three metres in diameter, but sometimes as a complete circle. Many of the stones may have slid

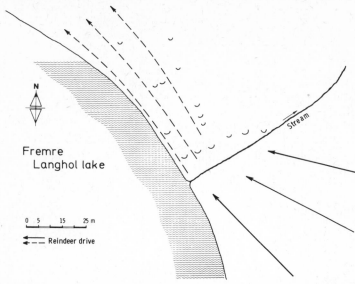

N

Fremre
Langhol lake

0 5   15   25 m

<=== Reindeer drive

Stream

Fig. 8. The archers most often have had a short distance when shooting the animals.

Fig. 9. A reduced and presumably very old hide for archers. A rucksack, as well as the white line indicate the dimension.

out of position and if it is especially old, the hide can have an appearance as in Fig. 9. When the formation is reduced as much as this, a connection to other hides is required before an interpretation can be advanced.

31

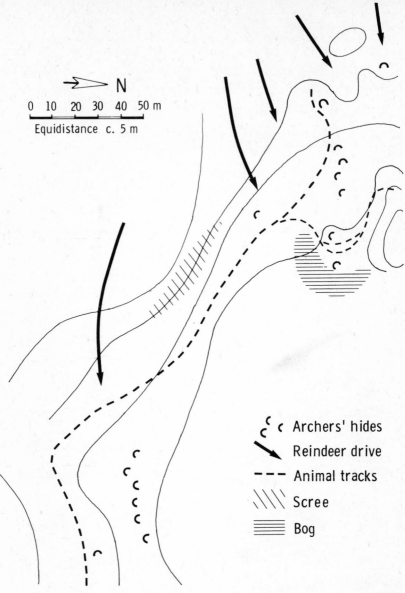

N

0 10 20 30 40 50 m

Equidistance c. 5 m

$\begin{smallmatrix}c\\c\end{smallmatrix}$ c Archers' hides

Reindeer drive

Animal tracks

Scree

Bog

Fig. 10. A system of hides for shooting where the terrain formations are utilized.

The hunters have very often used the reindeer's natural tendency to run up hills when they are frightened. Fig 10 shows such a situation where the animals would choose their instinctive running routes, resulting in shooting chances for the archers.

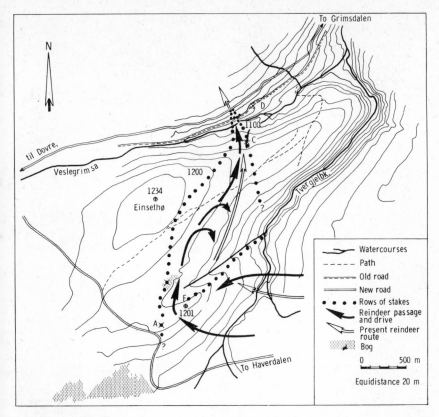

Fig. 11. On Einsethø, 10 km northwest of Rondane National Park, there is a trapping arrangement utilizing a combination of the reindeer's natural routes and the result of frightening the animals.

Trapping of many animals at the same time in large arrangements

Remains of five ancient trapping constructions, built to capture and kill a large number of reindeer at one time, have been found in the Rondane area in central Norway (Barth 1977). One of them, at Einsethø west of Grimsdalen, is of special interest because of the many finds of remains of wooden poles from a funnel construction.

Einsethø is at the same time the largest of such constructions near Rondane. It is funnel- or V-shaped with converging sides 2750 m long (Fig. 11). Nowadays fairly small cairns can be seen about 3 m apart, originally containing poles placed in regular lines (Fig. 12). In boggy areas tree stumps are found instead of cairns, and in other places where

Fig. 12. Part of one of the converging rows of stones or cairns, originally holding stakes on Einsethø.

34

holes could be dug, marked stone arrangements for holding the stakes are found. It would not have been necessary to have rope between the poles, since in the treeless area the stakes themselves would be sufficiently frightening. No hides for archers have been found in the whole arrangement.

It must have been hard work to set up and maintain this large construction, consisting of at least 1700 stakes, which may have been 1.5–2 m high, requiring approx. 3000 m of timber. The longest pole found in wet moss beside a stream is today 1.56 m long. All remains of poles found are of pine, and today one needs to travel 10 km from Einsethø to obtain pine usable wood.

Remains of five poles are dated to the period c. A.D. 980–1200. This confirms that the construction may have been in use until around the Black Death in 1349. The arrangement is found at an altitude of about 1000–1200 m. Nowadays pine is found here up to an altitude of about 900 m, while birch trees exist up to about 1000 m. During the Viking Age the tree line could not have been especially higher than today.

The reindeer routes are in the direction shown by arrows (Fig. 11). The opening A–F is 300 m wide, and when a sufficient number of animals have passed, a couple of guards were probably positioned here. The valley formed by the stream Tvergjelbekk is steeply-sloped and difficult to cross. The eastern line of cairns has not been identified further than to the question mark because of the rich shrub vegetation in the valley.

It is very interesting that the present main reindeer routes in this area pass exactly through the trapping construction and cross the stream Veslegrimsa just at the old slaughter place.

Fig. 13 shows the final part of the trap down the slope to Veslegrimsa and afterwards rising steeply to the actual place of capturing and killing (called P). At N tipping from the road has destroyed the details. It is thought that as soon as a herd of reindeer had passed the 16 m wide opening at M, it was closed with hunters. Hunters at N also frightened the animals, which now had no other way to run than towards P, where they were killed in the narrow pen. In the whole of this last section of the construction there must have been ropes or horizontal poles between the stakes, which at P were only 2 m apart. From the pen (P) it is 140 m along an old road to the settlement at D with the sites of three houses and where samples of charcoal and reindeer bones have been dug up. A few datings of charcoal, wood, and bones from these sites concern the period from about A.D. 600 to 1150 (Barth 1977: 28–29). So

35

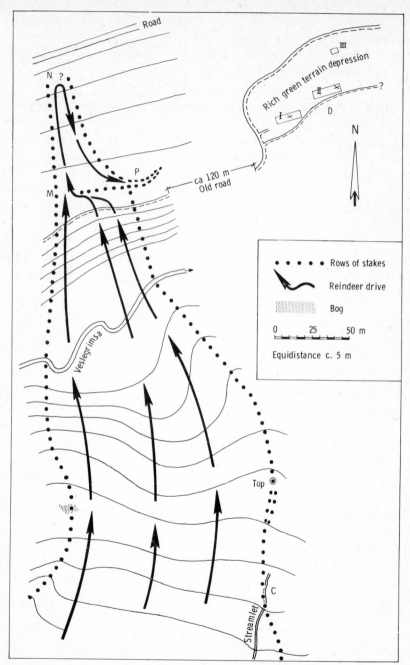

Fig. 13. *The final sprint on Einsethø before the killing into the slaughter pen P. The house sites I, II, III at D could not be seen from P.*

far we have no details from the settlement, since an archaeological excavation has not been undertaken.

Bløyvangen and Skjærilfjell within Rondane National Park have a hunting construction of the same type as on Einsethø, although of lesser extent (Barth 1977 p. 29 ff.). Lines of stakes, now seen as remains of cairns 3–5 m apart, up to 1250 m long, are arranged in a V-form with 56 hides for archers at strategic places.

Fig. 14 shows the last part of the converging rows with a steep upward slope from C to M, which flattens towards the end of the trap (i.e. the slaughter pen), where the stone cairns are about 2 m apart. Gaps in the line of cairns (formerly containing stakes) gave the animals a chance to break out, but many of these were shot from hides (C to M). Several hides are situated along the line of stakes, and it is clear that the shooting distance was often only a few metres. The breadth of these hides are between 1 and 3½ m. Some animals ran through to pen no. 1 at E (Fig. 14), but some may have turned, coming automatically into the second slaughter pen at F.

My theory is that both the slaughter pens consisted of solid pits of horizontally placed timber. The animals had to jump down into them and were immediately killed. At E there is a clear stone foundation for the ramp that the animals had to jump down from (Fig. 15). At F the terrain is naturally formed so that the animals fell sufficiently downwards into the timber pit. Nothing has yet been found giving any clue as to when this construction was in use, as all stakes were set in a dry and stony base, so there are no wooden remains. – In 1972 an iron arrowhead from A.D. 400–600 was found 500 m away from the slaughter pen.

The construction had about 600 stakes, on an average 3.3 m apart, requiring approx. 1000 m of timber. If all the 56 hides were in use at the same time, about a hundred people would be necessary for the whole arrangement. No settlement has yet been found.

Old reports of similar arrangements in Lappland in northern Scandinavia were given by Leem (1767), Tornæus (1772) and Fellman (1903/06), describing miles of converging fences for trapping wild reindeer this being particularly practised during the period 1500 until about 1700.

Richardson (1851: 393–394) refers to some Indians in arctic Canada who, in about 1840–1850, arranged a reindeer hunting system by means of 'two rows of stakes or trunks of trees extending for miles'. Hans Egede (1741) reported that in Greenland the Eskimos arranged a hunting system where the reindeer were forced to advance between two

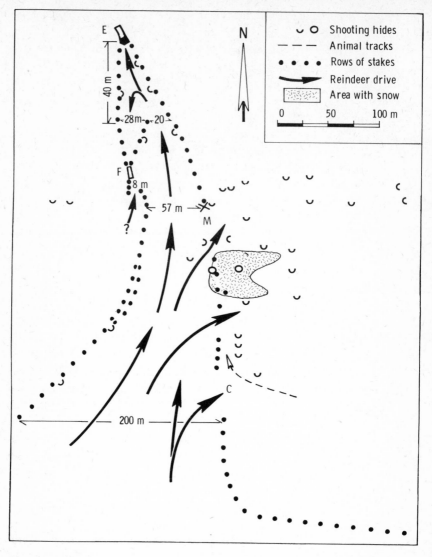

Fig. 14. The final sprint on Skaerilfjell with the slaughter pens nos. 1 (E) and 2 (F).

rows of light stakes with a bit of turf on top. Small stone cairns connected with rope were used in the same way. Ingstad (1951: 55–62) tells that the Nunamiut Eskimos in Alaska used at this time rows of cairns made of turf. He also found remains of older trapping arrangements which were similar to the converging fences in East Finnmark for distances of one km or more. The fences in Finnmark have often con-

Fig. 15. A possible situation at slaughter pen no. 1 at E (Fig. 14), seen towards NE. The stone foundation for the ramp (to the right) is clearly evident today (painted black in Fig. 14). Drawing by J. Nysæther.

sisted of single stones placed on edge (Vorren 1944, 1958 and 1969). A few years ago rock carvings, presumably from about 3500 years before Christ, were found in Alta in Finnmark showing many reindeer, moose, and one hunter encircled by a wooden-like fence (Helskog 1977).

On Hardangervidda in South Norway, there were stone cairns about 1 m high, which forced frightened reindeer to run into a lake, where they were killed. Bøe (1942: 21–24) points out leading fences on Hardangervidda. Later on, Blehr (1971 and 1973) describes similar arrangements where the animals were forced into the water near the Hardanger Glacier. He says (1973: 111) that radiological datings show that these constructions have been in use until the Black Death in 1349 and then became obsolete.

It seems to be a known point in Norway as well as in other arctic countries that both wild and domesticated reindeer, which have to be caught for killing or marking, will in the last part of the drive be forced to run up a steep slope. Then the terrain suddenly flattens and, at the same time, the animals have to enter the captivity pen. In just the same way the Eskimos had built up three or four ring-formed enclosures, one outside the other, with snares where the frightened animals were trapped (Ingstad 1951).

There are three other constructions in the Rondane area for capturing large numbers of reindeer at any one time (Barth 1977: 49 ff.). All these were based on driving the animals into a stony construction, which is clearly evident today. One of them, on Gravhø 1260 m a.s.l. (Fig. 16),

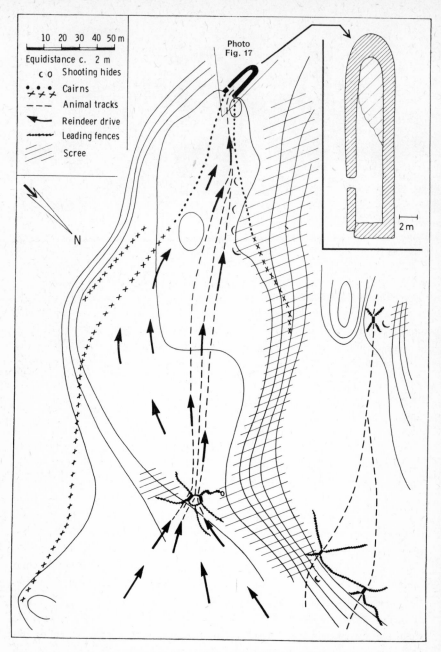

Fig. 16. *The trapping construction on Gravhø with detailed drawing (5 x enlarged) of the 19 m long and 3 m wide stone pen. Camera angle for Fig. 17 is shown. Five small pits with their leading fences are also marked.*

The labels within the figure:

10 20 30 40 50 m

Equidistance c. 2 m

c ᴏ   Shooting hides

Cairns

Animal tracks

Reindeer drive

Leading fences

Scree

N

Photo
Fig. 17

2 m

Fig. 17. The large stone pen on Gravhø, direction southwest.

has visible tracks leading towards the 19 m long stone pen, and small cairns in a V-formation that also lead to the pen. The shooting distance (from hides) may have been as short as about 2 metres. The rest of the running flock continued and could not see the trap because of a small hill, which they first had to pass; then they were too late to stop jumping down into a stony pen with almost 2 m high walls (Fig. 17). Five small pits for single animals are marked on the animal tracks (Fig. 16). These pits may have been in use at the same time as the larger construction, but it is most probable that they are more recent. A small bronze axe from 1000 to 1500 before Christ was found close to the construction in 1945.

In Engerdal in easternmost Norway (cf. Fig. 1) about 1100 m a.s.l. we have found a large trapping construction with stones standing on edge, about 40–70 cm high and 3–5 m apart (Fig. 18) (S. & E .K. Barth 1981).

This is a large arrangement with many rows of stones, the longest

Fig. 18. Stones standing on edge form the arms in the converging arrangement. Mountain Rendalssølen in the background.

approx. 1800 m (A–B, Fig. 19). Some sections of the rows must have been formed by wooden stakes resulting in different kinds of funnels and single rows for turning around the frightened animals in connection with different wind directions. If possible, frightened reindeer will always run against rising ground and against the wind. When the animals came up the hill towards Storhøa the stones rose up against the sky, and we have seen that it is impossible at this distance to calculate how large the stones are. The stones look like human beings. At the same time some archers would have been sitting in hides close to the stones. Towards point B the animals would have been running at a very high speed, and where the construction ends there is suddenly a big stony scree completely immobilizing the animals. – A total of 36 hides for archers have been found.

With wind from west or southwest the arrangements on Buhøgda–Buehøgda came into use. It is possible that rows of stakes from C to D have been taken away when the trap was not in use. It may be that a large annual migration of reindeer has taken place which minimized the time of hunting. Many people must have been involved in this hunting, and it is thought that the construction is very old. We have no proof to show where these people have lived, and so far we have no facts as to when they lived. All the stakes seem to have been placed in a dry and

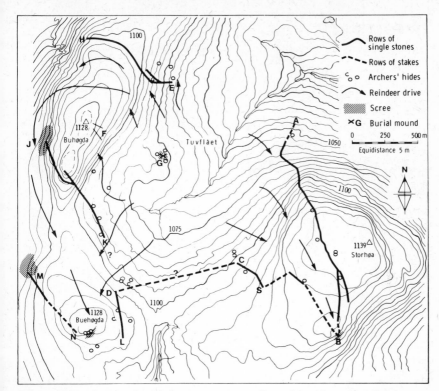

Fig. 19. Map showing the whole construction in Engerdal with many rows of stones on edge and presumed wooden stakes.

stony base, so no wooden remains have been found. In c. 1932 an iron weapon knife, 42 cm long, was found 1200 m southeast of the top of Storhøa. It is from c. A.D. 600–700.

Acknowledgements

I am very thankful to my wife, Sonja, who has always been a very interested and valuable assistant during a hard field-work. Financial support has been given by the Norwegian Research Council for Science and Humanities and by the Norwegian Forestry Museum, Elverum and is very much appreciated. The diagram drawings have been made by M. B. Ranheim of the University of Oslo. (All the photographs were taken by the author.)

Summary

Pitfalls with vertical walls built of stone approx. 2 m deep and approx. 2 x 0.7 m wide, with low stone fences leading to the four corners may have been a phenomenon peculiar to the southern Norwegian high mountains.

C 14-datings of wooden remains give the final period of their use up to c. A.D. 1600–1700, but most stopped being used about A.D. 1200–1300 in the Rondane mountains.

Another and more widespread type of pitfall in the lower mountains is described as a ring-formed depression in the earth, originally supported by a wooden construction. In Rondane they have been used during the whole period after Christ to c. A.D. 1500–1600. One C 14-dating in such a pit outside Rondane indicates that the initial period for its use may have occurred c. 4500 years B.C.

Hides for archers with bows and arrows are mentioned, sometimes in connection with large trapping constructions, where cairns, poles or stones on edge are found in converging rows of up to 2–3 km. Four of six arrangements of this kind are described, one of them with a series remains of poles from c. A.D. 980–1200.

Bibliography

Bang-Andersen, S. & Kjos-Hanssen, O.
    1979 På spor etter de første mennesker i høyfjellet. Pp. 31–45 in Arkeol. Mus. Stavanger. Småtr. 3. 139 pp.

Barth, E. K.
    1974 Gamle fangstanlegg for rein og elg. Statsskog årg. 10: 34–46. Oslo.
    1975 Stone-sided reindeer pitfalls in Jämtland. (In Norwegian with English summary.) Norsk Skogbruksmus. årb. 7: 113–120. Elverum.
    1977 The mass trapping of wild reindeer in the Rondane mountains. (In Norwegian with English summary.) Norsk Skogbruksmus. årb. 8: 9–74. Elverum.
    1979 Reindeer pitfalls in Rondane and other mountains. (In Norwegian with English summary.) Pp. 139–148 in Fortiden i søkelyset. 283 pp. Lab. Radiolog. Dat. Trondheim.
    1981a Reindeer and elk, vital resources throughout millennia. (In Norwegian with English summary.) Fauna 34: 150—161. Oslo.
    1981b Hunting pits in Forest Areas. (In Norwegian with English summary.) Norsk Skogbruksmus. årb. 9: 272—298. Elverum.

Barth, E. K., Lima de Faria, A. & Berglund, B. E.
    1980 Two 14C dates of wood samples from Rondane, Norway. Bot. Notiser 133: 643–644. Stockholm.

Barth, S. & E. K.
1981 Trapping construction for wild reindeer on Storhøa in Engerdal. (In Norwegian with English summary.) Norsk Skogbruksmus. årb. 9: 260–271. Elverum.

Blehr, Otto
1971 Noen fornminner og sagn fra Hardangerviddas fangstliv. Viking 34 (1970): 89–103.
1973 Traditional Reindeer Hunting and Social Change in the Local Communities Surrounding Hardangervidda. Norwegian Archeol. Rev. 6: 102–112.

Burch, E. S.
1972 The Caribou/Wild Reindeer as a Human Resource. American Antiquity 37: 339–368.

Bøe, Johs.
1942 Til Høgfjellets forhistorie. Bergens Mus. skr. 21: 1–96.

Egede, Hans (1741)
1926 Grønlands beskrivelse. A. W. Brøgger, Oslo.

Fellman, Jacob
1903/06 Anteckningar under min vistelse i Lappmarken. Vols. I–IV. Helsinki.

Helskog, Knut
1977 Et reingjerde fra steinalderen. Ottar 101: 25–29.

Ingstad, Helge
1951 Nunamiut. Blant Alaskas innlandseskimoer. Gyldendal. Oslo.

Leem, Knud
1767 Beskrivelse over Finnmarkens Lapper. Copenhagen.

Middendorff, A.v.
1875 Reise in den äussersten Norden und Osten Sibiriens während der Jahre 1843 und 1844. IV, 2. St. Petersburg.
1953 Auf Schlitten, Boot und Renntierrücken. Brockhaus Verlag. Leipzig.

Moe, D., Indrelid, S. & Kjos-Hanssen, O.
1978 A study of environment and early man in the southern Norwegian highlands. Norwegian Archeol. Rev. 11: 73–83. .

Mølmen, Øystein
1976 Viltbiologiske forundersøkelser i Jotunheimen/Breheimen. Felt 2. Fangst og jakt på villrein. 212 pp. NVE. Statskraftverkene. Oslo.
1977 Viltbiologiske forundersøkelser i Jotunheimen/Breheimen. Felt 1, 3, 4 og 5. Fangst og jakt på villrein. 244 pp. NVE. Statskraftverkene. Oslo.
1978 Villreinen i Snøhetta-feltet. 497 pp. Direktor. Vilt og Ferskv.fisk – Viltforskningen. Trondheim.

Nilsson, S.
1847 Skandinavisk Fauna. I. Däggdjuren. 2. oppl. 656 pp. Lund.

Øverland, O. A.
1893 Illustrert Norges Historie bd. VI. Folkebladets Forl., Kristiania.

Paus, Halvor
1973 Dyregravenes økonomiske betydning og om et fangstanlegg ved inngangen til Jutulhogget. Norsk Veterinærtids. 85: 11–13.

Proudfoot, V. B.
1967 Experiments in archaeology. Science Journ. 3 (11): 59–64.

Reusch, Hans
1897 Dyregravene i høifjeldet. Norsk Jæger & Fiskerforen. Tids. 26: 1–3.

Richardson, John
1851 Arctic Searching Expedition. Journal of a Boat Voyage through Ruperts Land and the Arctic Sea. Bd. I. 413 pp. London.

Selinge, K.-G.
1974 Fångstgropar. Fornvårdaren 12. 39 pp. Jämtlands läns museum.
Tornæus, Johannes
1772 Beskrifning öfver Tornå ock Kemi Lappmarker. Förf. 1672. 68 pp. Stockholm.
Vorren, Ørnulv
1944 Dyregraver og reingjerder i Varanger. S. 1–99 i Bidrag til finnernes bygdehistorie og etnografi bd. 2. Nord-norske samlinger VI. Etnografisk museum, Oslo.
1958 Samisk villreinfangst i eldre tid. Ottar 17: 1–42.
1969 Undersøkelser over villreinfangstanlegg i Norges samestrøk. Norrbotten: 125–144. Norrb. Museums årsb.
Wold, Johan
1929 En gammel drapssak om fiskeretten i Mår. Dyrestupene i Mårsnås. Litt om stupveidingen. Norsk Jæger & Fiskerforen. Tids. 58: 142–147.

Conditions for Hunting at the Stalo Sites

Rolf Kjellström

In the Swedish Laplandic area there are a particular kind of culture-remains called Stalo sites. These sites are usually of an oval shape with a lowered bottom plane encompassed by a wall.

The Stalo sites are obviously remains of some sort of housing, but whether or not these have been the dwelling places of tame reindeer herdsmen or wild reindeer hunters can be discussed. It may therefore be of a certain interest to have a closer look at the actual locations of the Stalo sites, particularly in relation to hunting.

Five of the six groups of Stalo sites which, in this respect, shall be accounted for here, have been discovered in connection with the intensive inventory work carried out by Nordiska museet under my guidance in the Sarek-Padjelanta district within the parish of Jokkmokk 1973–77. One group of Stalo sites has earlier been described and registered by Ernst Manker. The six groups contain altogether 13 Stalo sites. Their location in relation to hunting will be described one by one in the following, with their respective number as registered with the Ancient Monument register at the Royal Office of National Antiquities (*Riksantikvarieämbetet*).

No 415:

The Stalo sites at Sallohaure are situated in the eastern part of a land area between large mountain lakes. In addition they are located in the proximity of a hunting pit system, earlier registered by Manker, containing six pits and forming a barrier across the wedge of land called Njunjes between Sallohaure and Vuojatätno. According to Manker a widespread reindeer grazing ground has here its funnel-shaped mouth for the reindeer paths eastwards.

The hunting pit system constitutes, according to Manker, a typical

47

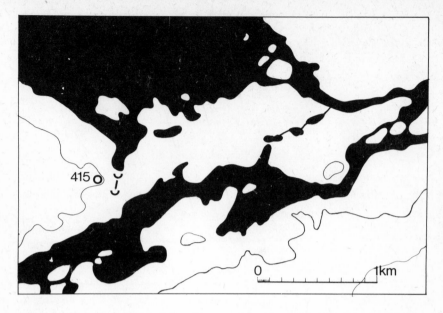

example of such a system's location, and he also adds that one could have expected an even larger system here (Manker 1960: 68 ff.).

If one regards the hunting pit system as the basis for hunting in this area, it is possible that the hunting has taken place mainly from the west, but also from the east. It is also possible that reindeer can have been hunted close to where the tongue of land is bordered by water in the north, east and west.

No 424:

The centre of the hunting area has probably consisted of a narrow passage, where it would have been natural for the reindeer to pass. In the north the area is bordered by Låutakjauratj and a smaller lake beside it, which in turn is surrounded by a narrow stretch of land. There is also a small brook between Låutakjåkkå and Låutakjauratj, which could cause trouble for the reindeer. The brook looks innocent enough, but it is deep and makes the passage more difficult, although it cannot be seen as a very great obstacle. In the south the passage is made more difficult by the large and mighty Låutakjåkkå, which the reindeer prefer not to encounter. The passage earlier mentioned, between lakes and brooks, does not seem narrow at a distance, for which reason the reindeer do not hesitate to pass there.

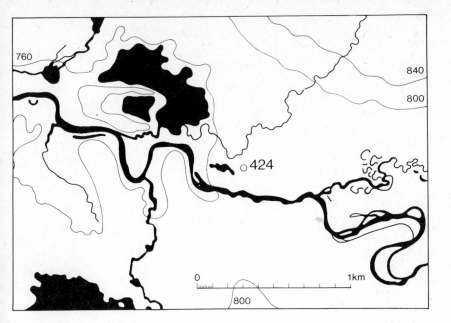

Battue can here preferably have taken place both from the west and the east.

The Stalo sites concerned by the above-described hunting situation have earlier been recorded by Manker (Manker 1960: 273 ff.).

No 435:

The Stalo sites at Rapukmålke are situated at the confluence of two brooks, i e Låddejåkkå and Pårajåkåtj. In the vicinity of the Stalo sites Låddejåkkå makes a sharp turn and forms in this way an obstacle on two sides.

One can imagine that the hunting has taken place either from the northwest or from the east. It cannot, however, have been very profitable from the south sides of the brooks.

No 462:

In my opinion, the Stalo sites here have a connection with three existing groups of hunting pits, consisting of 11, 1, and 3 respectively, which have been dug in a reindeer path along a ridge running northwest–southeast.

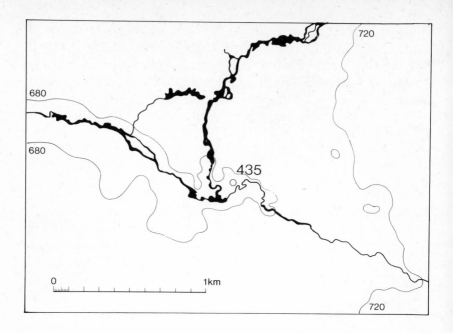

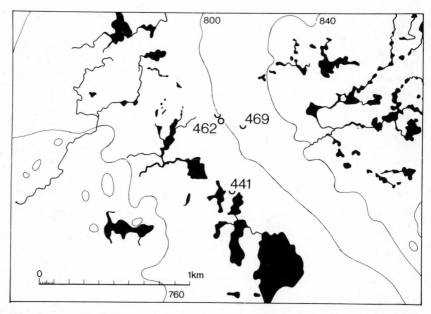

The reason for believing that the reindeer have wandered in the same main direction as the ridge rests on the fact that north and south of the ridge there are two areas with a lot of small lakes and watercourses.

50

According to this way of reasoning one can suppose, not without reservation though, that tame reindeer and wild reindeer have wandered along the same paths. This matter is, however, so complex that it ought to be a subject for a more thorough investigation. For certain reasons, which I shall not enter into here, there are however circumstances that imply that wild reindeer and tame reindeer resemble each other in the way they wander.

No 846:

The hunting situation at the Stalo sites at Sierkavagge is limited by watercourses: in the west by one running north-south, Spietjaujåkkå; in the north, northeast, and east, by Sierkajåkkå, which here is wider; in the south and southeast, by small lakes. These watercourses form a triangular shaped area. The heights in the south and northwest of the small lakes emphasize the instinct of the reindeer to move towards the wedge-shaped area around the Stalo sites. It has probably been best to undertake battue from the south and possibly also from the west.

No 1025:

Stalo site 1025 is also situated in the vicinity of a confluence of different watercources: Spietjaujåkkå (southeast of the Stalo site), Njerekjåkåtj (south of the Stalo site), and a nameless brook (immediately north of the Stalo site).

With these watercourses as a starting point, there are different areas suitable for hunting:

I West of the confluence of Spietjaujåkkå and the nameless brook.

II Southwest of the junction of Spietjaujåkkå and Njerekjåkåtj.

III West of the confluence of Njerekjåkåtj and the brook with the still-water (southwest of the Stalo site).

The most suitable direction from which to hunt would be:

For area   I: from west-southwest.
  ”   ”   II: from the south along Spietjaujåkkå.
  ”   ”   III: from southwest to northeast along the western side of Njerekjåkåtj.

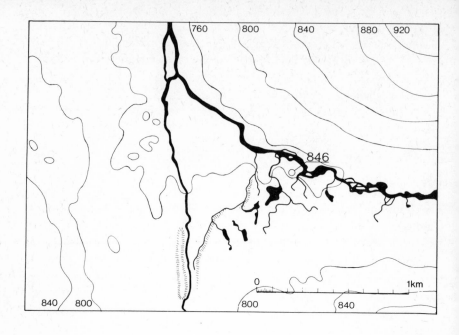

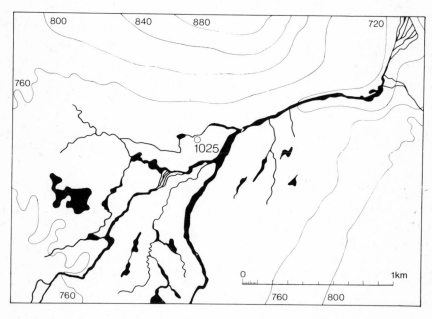

Conclusion

The above-presented interpretations of the hunting situation at the Stalo sites do not constitute proof of its having been the way I have described.

All of the above-mentioned groups of Stalo sites can be said to have an ideal location in relation to the routes of the reindeer and also from the point of view of the reindeer herdsmen. Consequently the Stalo sites can also have been dwellings for the reindeer herdsmen.

However, I rather think that the Stalo sites have been headquarters for hunters. On condition that the wild reindeer have wandered in about the same way as the tame reindeer, the Stalo sites have also had, from the point of view of hunting, a very favourable location. The existence of five hunting-pit systems, or groups of hunting-pit systems, at three of the six groups of Stalo sites, also brings to mind the idea of hunting.

Five of the six groups of Stalo sites have similar locations, i e in the proximity of confluences of different brooks or close to meeting places of brook/brooks and lakes. The sixth group has a connection with three existing hunting-pit systems in its immediate vicinity. This system of pits is in turn situated in an area bordered on two sides by routes containing a lot of lakes.

It is my opinion that places such as the ones here described – at confluences of different brooks and lake systems, as well as areas with hunting-pit systems, can have been centres for battue of wild reindeer.

All the larger brooks in the area of investigation, selected by Nordiska museet in the Sarek-Padjelanta district, are situated in the vicinity of the Stalo sites.

The inhabitants of the Stalo sites can indeed have lived in the mountains for different reasons and purposes. In this area it seems, however, as if hunting has been of a major importance as a source of living.

Bibliography

Manker, E.
1960 Fångstgropar och stalotomter. Acta Lapponica XV. Stockholm.

The Wild Reindeer Hunt and Offering Sites

Ørnulf Vorren

When it was suggested that this symposium be held in the Tromsø area, the rationale was, among other things, that in this region there are cultural remains from the time of hunters and gatherers which are recognizable and readily demonstrative for the symposium's participants. Even today, the economy of the area in large measure takes into account the basic industries of hunting and fishing.

It was in fact hunting and fishing which, some hundreds of years ago, provided the basis for the old Saami hunting and gathering culture. The wild reindeer population was one of the most important resources exploited by these hunting and gathering Saamis. In fact, one can say that reindeer was the most significant of all the land mammals to be hunted. The progressive decline of this wild reindeer stock, starting from around 1500 to 1600, was one of the significant factors in the differentiation of the hunting and gathering culture into reindeer nomadism and another distinctive coastal-and-inland culture within the Saami settlement area.

Literary documentation of Saami wild reindeer hunting already exists from around A.D. 890 in the record made by King Alfred the Great of a visitor named Ottar from Hålogaland. Ottar claims to have six reindeer decoys which were very valuable for Saamis in the wild reindeer hunt. This trait was not only characteristic of Saamis, for among hunting and gathering cultures across the entire northern Eurasian continent, reindeer breeding has buttressed the other subsistence activities of hunting, trapping, fishing and gathering.

The wild reindeer hunt finds much more concrete documentation in the forests and fells throughout the Saami hunting territories. Even today we can identify innumerable remains from pitfall systems and hunting barricades for the now non-existent wild reindeer. We also find the living sites occupied during the hunting season for wild reindeer.

Most of the registered remains from this hunting system are marked on the map, Fig. 1. Besides these there is naturally a large but unknown number that have not been registered. Among other things, we have not

Fig. 1.

included the Kola peninsula, where such hunting constructions were commonly employed.

We have unfortunately not found many of the living sites that were used during the wild reindeer hunt. One we have studied consists of 15 sodhut foundations surrounded by piles of reindeer antler and bone. Cultural material from this site consists of bone and iron tools. Iron tools were in the topmost layers and included lanceheads and arrowpoints, knives, and so on, everything pertinent to use in the hunt. In association with the hunting structures, both around the pitfalls and near the other kinds of hunting constructions, corrals and fences, there are numerous cache pits in the stony slopes or in accumulated mounds of flagstone. These have been used to preserve the catch. To judge from the number of these meat caches, the number of animals caught must have been considerable, even though one must assume that it could vary from year to year.

There are unfortunately no remains of hunting corrals and fences from the wild reindeer hunt in the symposium's excursion area. Therefore I will only briefly mention them there. Hunting corrals and fences in the Saami area have been investigated only on the Varanger peninsula, where in all eight such constructions have been described. Their main feature of construction is that two rows of stone, stone pillars, and fences of stone are arranged so that the rows begin some distance from each other, then gradually approach each other to form a funnel which opens out into a slaughtering site. This can lie along a cliff, in a talus or scree field, in a lake or water system, and finally in an enclosure, a corral, usually round in form and situated higher up, preferably around a hillock. This form of hunting with corrals and fences can be found described in a number of archival records. Some of these concern just those remains which now exist on the Varanger peninsula. In addition there are several so-called hunting maze-rings or archer's blinds where one has overtaken the wild reindeer and surprised them with a fatal lance, arrow, or bullet. Judging from documentary sources, this type of hunting went out sometime in the middle of the 1600's.

Hunting by means of pitfall systems presumably pre-dates that with corral/fences (Fellman 1906: 58). As mentioned, pits from these extensive systems are found throughout the entire territory occupied by the old hunting and gathering Saami culture. They lie in successions of rows. The pits are generally oval with their longer dimension perpendicular to that of the row.

Between the pits were fences of logs and branches, and in this way there was a gate for each pitfall. When prepared for use, each pit was covered with thin branches on a frame of more solid wooden poles. On top as camouflage there had been laid moss, heath and twigs.

All of these corral/fences and pitfall systems are found in places referred to by Saamis as 'suoppaš'. These are places where reindeer generally pass, for example, tongues of land between watercourses, fording localities, drier parts of a marsh, along rivers and lakes – especially where the passage between the shore and a mountain wall is narrow – and, finally, over watersheds or divides. These last-mentioned form crossings, as it were, for the migratory routes of the reindeer, for they must be traversed by the herd whether it is wandering from mountain to mountain or from the end of a valley or a river-bed over to another on the other side of a mountain.

Throughout the hunting territory of the hunting and trapping Saamis one can today find remains from another, and not unimportant, aspect of the hunt. As we know, hunting and trapping has been associated with magic down through the ages. We find concrete expressions of this from the stone age rock carvings down to the more abstract practices today, when, for example, the sportsman spits on the hook before casting it out. One is out after good luck in the catch, much as is the hope of those who see off the fishermen with the cry of 'Tvi-tvi'.

Among hunting and trapping Saamis this type of magic was probably of a much more serious character. Luck in hunting was among the central themes in their mythology, their religion, and their magical rituals. Therefore one almost always finds offering sites or 'seidi' of various descriptions in association with remains from the large hunting systems. These are often enclosed with a stone fence in a circle of six to nine metres in diameter. An offering place of stone or wood stood inside on an elevated site. Sacrificial gifts were placed here.

In the symposium's excursion area, there are pitfall systems arranged along the various types of 'suoppaš' passages in the reindeer migration routes mentioned above.

At the head of Storfjord, which is the inner part of the larger Lyngenfjord, a valley opens from the west with steep slopes from the high mountain complex to the north and south. The watercourse system here has its shed far to the west with a corresponding river in a valley which leads west to the head of Balsfjord. This relatively narrow strip of land between the heads of the two large fiords creates a passage area – a grand 'suoppaš', if you will – for the long wild reindeer migrations from the interior and out over the peninsula between the two fiords in the spring and back again in the autumn. In both of the extended valleys east and west of the watershed mentioned, there lie rows and rows of pits on the sand and gravel terraces along the valley-sides and out on the river plain.

We will inspect closer one pitfall system in the valley to the east of the watershed, here called Oterdalen. Side valleys join this valley from the south and north. There are several pitfall systems in Oterdalen, but we choose one of them which seems to lend itself best to illustrating its situation in relation to the large reindeer migration route over the valley

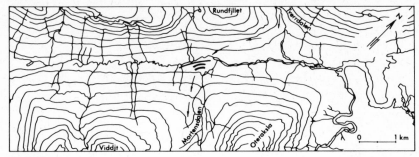

Fig. 2.

from the mountains in the north to the fell complexes in the south. The
pitfall system lies at the mouth of the side valley, Mortensdalen. (See
the map, Fig. 2.) The stream in this valley has cut a deep gully as it
gushed out over the valley-side. On the west side of this gully and
stream, the foothills stretch from the valley-side toward the river in
gently sloping plains.

In the course of time the river has cut out several river terraces. It
is upon these moors that we find the pits from a relatively large pitfall
system. Along the edge toward the river plain lies a row of pits, which
extends several kilometres up the valley beyond the moors on the west
side of the stream in Mortensdal. Fifty to a hundred metres above, on
the edge of the hill, lies a corresponding system such that the two pitfall systems form a double-rowed obstruction in the area. We must now
assume that there have been mounds or barricades of poles and branches
between the pits.

Unfortunately Highway E 6 swings between the two systems and has
probably also destroyed some pits. In any case, it somewhat disturbs
the picture of the landscape as it must have been when intact. Nevertheless, there must have been a passageway for wild reindeer herds here
over the valley, a 'suoppaš', where there has also been loose material
suitable for pit-digging. The setting indicates that the reindeer must
have been moving along the valley in order to gain access to the mountain complex in the south. Precisely here, along the south side of the
valley, there is a more gradual slope up the valley-side west of the stream
in Mortensdal between the mountains of Oter-aksla and Viddjet. Above
the steep valley-side, Mortensdal stretches broad and flat over toward
the next valley that the migration will take, Signaldalen.

As one views the north side of Oterdalen, it rises fairly steeply 500
to 600 metres up toward Rundfjellet. A little hanging valley just south

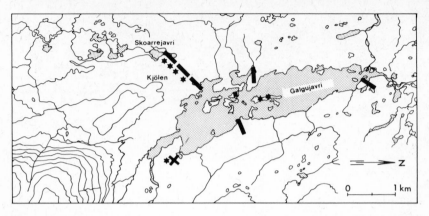

Fig. 3.

of the mountain eases the slope above 300 metres, but all the same the stretch does not give the impression of being designed for a migration route. On the other hand, two or three kilometres directly north of the hunting complex, there is a valley, Tverrdalen, which leads from the mountains in the north down Oterdalen. It is likely that here the wild reindeer have drawn on their fall migration from summer pastures to winter range. In that case, as indicated by the arrow on the map, Fig. 2, the animals will have moved down the south side of Tverrdalen and then followed the foothills south until they have reached the river, crossed the fords above the mouth of the stream in Mortensdal, and entered the terraces on the south side of it, in order to ascend on the west side of the afore-mentioned gully in Mortensdal and into the broad and flat valley passage to the south.

But along the way the reindeer have encountered the constructions between the pitfalls, found the openings, and been trapped in the pits. Perhaps one might imagine that instead the animals came from the south, down the valley-side and forward on the terrace edges to the pitfalls. But in that case one must take into consideration that the hunt took place in the autumn and then the reindeer were on migration to the south. There are correspondingly designed pitfall systems in other localities. Strategically, one can also imagine that it is advantageous for the animals to advance into the constructions on their way up the hill. In such an ascending approach they cannot see the detours at a distance and can more easily come into the openings where the pitfalls lie. One finds the same principle applied in the hunting corrals/fences where the corridors or funnels lead up the hillside.

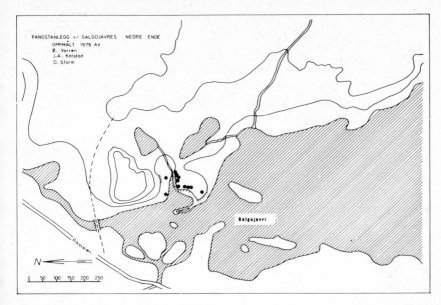

Galgujavri

N

0 50 100 150 200 250

Fig. 4.

The following examples of remains from pitfall construction are taken from the region around Galgujavri (see map, Fig. 3), which was included in the symposium's excursion. Galgujavri is a lake which lies very near 'Kjølen', the basic watershed between the Skibotn drainage system, leading down to Lyngenfjord, and the Muonio drainage system, which leads down toward the Tornio river and ends in the Gulf of Bothnia.

Near Galgujavri, which is the second-highest lake-source for the Skibotn drainage system, there lie remains from three pitfall systems situated along three different kinds of 'suoppaš' passage areas. As soon as one comes near the outlet from the lake along the highway from Skibotn to Galgujavri, there are two points of land which stick out from each side of the lake opposite each other. On both sides of these are several various-sized islands. The lake is quite shallow here (before damming). Conditions are consequently favourable for migrating reindeer herds to cross the lake and for this to be a fording point.

To the east of the lake one also finds remains from a pitfall system with a total of 11 pits. It is clear that here one has had an obstruction of the crossing over the lake. (See Fig. 4.) That the row of pits is not continuous furthest toward the south, correlates with there being so little loose material that it has not been possible to construct pits. One must assume that there has been a sturdy fence, which has led the animals north to the pitfalls. The animals must have then come migrating from the north on the west side of the Galgujokk-valley from the mountain area near Vardo and Rieppe. They have consequently followed the relatively easy terrain filled with bog and water which leads to Sallujavri and Sallujokka's outlet into Galgujavri. They have here reached the afore-mentioned ford over to the headland on the east side of the lake and have been trapped by the constructions enclosing the pitfalls.

The next crossing point lies roughly in the middle of Galgujavri. Here are numerous islets and points of land which nearly fill up the central part of the lake. Here one can visualize two passages, one to the north over a couple of islets and one just south of this with a passage from the east side toward a hooked point which sticks out on the west side, or vice versa. (See Fig. 3.) Here the migration can have come both ways – from the mountains in the north on the *east* side of Galgujokk-valley and along Galgujavri from the region in the north on the *west* side of Galgujavri. In each case the migration can have proceeded on to the south aiming toward the appropriate passage for crossing 'Kjølen'. On these two 'suoppaš' crossings, one does not find very many depressions from pitfall construction, but those which are there seem on balance to be situated at extremely strategic points. On the east side one has blocked the passage along the foothill and the lake in the form of a row of pits. On the west side one finds several pits more or less opposite those on the east side, and finally there is a single pit on the constriction of a headland. These pits are arranged so that they can trap the animals right on their own paths to and from the lake.

The barriers on the east side of the lake can have served both to trap the animals and to lead them to the crossing via the islands and headland.

It is evident that the two crossings with their pitfall constructions all lie on the route to the truly large hunting grounds, the passage over the large watershed, the 'Kjølen' divide. This lies on the depression between Salluoai'vi and the lower Båssuvarri in the northwest and on the other side Jiekašoai'vi in the southeast. This 'suoppaš' lies about 500 metres beneath the highest of the mountain complexes on either side.

The distance between the Galgujavri and Muonio drainage system's highest source toward the watershed and Skoarrejavri in Silasvuobme is only 1000 metres in a straight line. The area here is partially filled with moraine materials between stone crags and large scree fields of loose rocks. The scree areas consist for the most part of large and small dead ice depressions. (See Fig. 5.) Inasmuch as these scree fields are very difficult to traverse, they constitute, on the one hand, natural barriers

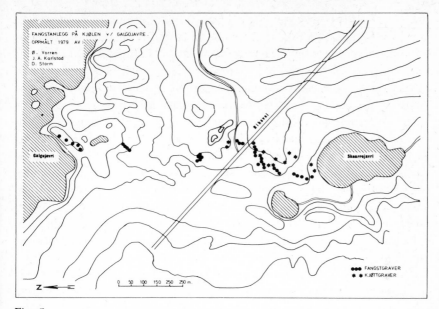

Galgujavri

Skoarrejavri

Z

0   50 100 150 250 250 m.

●●● FANGSTGRAVER
★ ★ KJØTTGRAVER

Fig. 5.

for migrating reindeer, while on the other hand they are well designed for the ambush of animals wandering into them.

For the hunt, this 'suoppaš' seems to be ideal, strategically speaking. Here one is at the lowest point of the large watershed. On both sides there are relatively broad basins with stunted deciduous woods along the moraine ridges and with small marshes along streams and lakes. The wild reindeer migration route must have passed here from Galgujavri over to the Silas drainage system, which leads down to the Muonio valley. But the migration can also have traversed this 'suoppaš' from Båssuvarri in the northwest to Jiekašvarri in the southeast. In both instances, the little stretch of about half a square kilometre has been in the natural crossing. The hunting folk have noted these conditions and used the area as their hunting grounds. The map (Fig. 6) indicates this area between Galgujavri in the north and the small Skoarrejavri in the south. Every single pitfall, 35 in all, is situated between a point of land in the former and the upper end of the latter. The map also indicates with a separate symbol in all 10 pits for the preservation of the catch. These pits or meat caches have been constructed in a scree field by removing enough stone for the placement of two or three reindeer carcasses, which are then heaped with rocks.

In the course of the investigations here, one such cache, which appeared untouched, was opened. At the bottom of the pit were the bones of two shoulders, two thighs, and some vertebrae of reindeer. Everything was packed inside – a plastic sack. This old meat cache, laying near several opened caches, was itself used for its original purpose even in the plastic age. The meat that had been on the bones had naturally disintegrated or been consumed by mice, ants, or other creatures.

From the situation of the pitfalls one can conclude that hunting in the area has taken place in the fall or in late summer when the reindeer have been migrating southwards. The animals have entered the hunting grounds where the large scree fields begin and where the pitfall systems are placed. (See Fig. 5.) If they approached from the lower area along the west side of Galgujavri, they would meet the barrier with the three pitfall complexes which lie in the north. Here is also the most extensive collection of loose scree stone. If they came further south from the mountains in the northwest and over Båssuvarri, they would have most likely encountered the hunting area with the rows of pitfalls in the south. The approach to the rows of pits here leads over some gravel flats covered with deciduous woods, heath and moss. But where the pits lie in a depression toward the south, the bouldered ridge is bare, and the pits lie along the edge of the boulder field. Therefore, many of the pits have been constructed by heaving out rocks which then lie with gravel and sand in a bank around the pits.

The row of pits ends near the little Skoarrejavri. The reindeer can of course have swum over this lake. But this has scarcely been the case when the animals cannot be assumed to have been driven toward the hunting grounds, but to have approached the watershed either while browsing or walking at an easy tempo.

Even though the pitfalls can hardly have been in shape for use at other seasons than autumn, there may have been trapping or hunting with accumulated stone as a blind for the hunter. However, remains from such devices have not yet been found which could indicate this.

It has been mentioned above that, in connection with the wild reindeer hunt as well as for other hunting, trapping, and fishing, one performed certain rituals at specifically designed locations to gain favour with the powers that be and to guarantee luck in the catch. There were several 'powers', to which one could address oneself in this respect. But the central hunting deity in Saami mythology is personified as 'Leib-ålbmai'. Such rituals have clearly also been carried out at Galgujavri. Here is namely an offering place of the type described above – a circular enclosure of stone. The location is indicated on the map, Fig. 3. It is

64

not contiguous to the hunting structures for wild reindeer which have been described, but rather on the other side of the river and at some distance from the south end of Galgujavri, where Gallajokka and Vægjetjokka have their outlets.

The offering site lies hidden here in a relatively disordered terrain. There are here, as there were in the hunting grounds, large scree fields, which lie in and around some large dead ice depressions. Consequently, there has been more than enough material for the construction of a stone wall. It is as distinctive as it is logical that where offering places of this type are found, they are situated in flat-stoned scree or in round boulder fields.

The offering site is placed between mounds of scree stone and moraines, which for the most part are overgrown with heath plants and moss and moreover covered with spread stunted birch. The stone enclosure itself has a maximum interior diameter of six metres and a corresponding exterior diameter of nine metres. The stone wall has now partially tumbled down but in places stands as originally constructed. The stones that have fallen from the top of the wall to both inside and outside the enclosure have made the present height of the wall relatively small.

The bottom of the enclosure inside the wall is made up of gravel and sand. Unfortunately, the original surface has been disturbed because some 'treasure seekers' have removed some of the gravel material. But the likelihood that there has been any 'altar-shaped' structure in the enclosure is at best slight. One can rather imagine that there have once stood wooden 'seide' here, as for example have existed at similar types of offering sites in several places in Finnmark. Wooden remains from any such 'seide' have not been found here. The site has not been excavated. Nor have there been found any wooden remains which may have been from a wooden extension on top of the stone wall. Nevertheless, such an extension is not unlikely, as they are known from several similar offering sites in Finnmark. At one of them, in the upper part of Karasjok valley, a five-sided extension of layers of wooden poles was built upon the stone wall.

Not far from the stone enclosure lie two depressions in the scree material. These have most likely been two meat caches. Similar pits are also found near other offering sites.

There can of course be some doubt as to whether the sacrificial site has been set up here in special connection with the wild reindeer hunt. The meat caches would indicate that carcasses of larger animals have been utilized in the sacrificial meal and as a sacrificial gift. However, it is characteristic that this type of offering site is generally found in areas also containing wild reindeer hunting complexes or in passages along their migration routes. Materials such as reindeer antler and bone around such offering places also confirm their function.

Now one could ask which group or groups of hunting and gathering folk once used the hunting complexes and the offering site which are described here?

If one first considers the pitfall system in Oterdalen, its position so close to the sea suggests that the pitfalls must have been used by a group that also had the fiord and ocean as resource areas. One can imagine that here it involves a hunting-and-trapping Saami pattern of resource utilization, where the head of the fiord has provided residence both winter and summer, where the subsistence activities associated with these seasons have been carried out. In the autumn, the surrounding valley and mountainous area has been the resource focus, and during the spring the object has possibly been fishing, sealing, and bird-snaring in the fiord and on the outlying islands. In this case one would have here a pattern of seasonally dispersed resources within the area of exploitation, as is well-documented in Finnmark from the closing phase of the hunting and trapping culture there.

When it concerns the Galgujavri region, the question is less clearcut. From archival research and the literature, one is more familiar with the hunting and gathering Saami band, or 'sii'da', which was just on the other side of the 'Kjølen' divide, namely the Rounala 'siida'. This siida's fishing lake lay directly on the south side of 'Kjølen'. It was clearly an inland group economically dependent on freshwater fishing in the drainage system and on hunting in the woods and on the fells. It was 80 kilometres from the fishing lakes near 'Kjølen' to their winter encampment far down in Muonio valley.

On the north side of 'Kjølen', another hunting Saami group or siida must have had its resource area. The fact is that it is not only near Galgujavri that one finds cultural remains from the hunting group's activities. Along the lakes and drainage systems in the mountains on both sides, there are remains of pitfalls, offering sites, and living sites.

There is no support for the possibility that the Rounala siida from the other side of 'Kjølen' could have extended its hunting area to this region. Moreover, from what we know about the territorial management in the last phase of the hunting and trapping culture, this is hardly likely. According to the general principles for the disposition of resource territory,

'Kjølen' should here either form a boundary or else a joint area where several *siida* groups have hunting grounds at various points on the periphery. Documentary sources provide some support for this when it concerns the so-called Jauris-duoddar in Finnmark, the watershed between Anarjokka/Karasjokka in the north and Ounasjoki/Kemijoki's sources in the south.

However, from archival materials no inland *siida* is known from the time of hunting and gathering culture north of the watershed in the Galgujavri region. Nor is it likely, judged ecologically, that a resource area here could satisfy access to subsistence needs in all seasons of the year. This would be the case especially during the winter and spring. While the mountain area has little to offer in the way of resources during these seasons, the fiord and coastal area is then particularly rich with potentialities. Hence, one can imagine that the Galgujavri area has been an autumn area for a *siida* of hunting Saamis which also has had the fiord and ocean as subsistence sources. It would be reasonable then for the head of the fiord, particularly Skibotn, to have been the winter residence. In fact, mounds exist here from an older settlement.

But this conclusion remains a working hypothesis. Continued fieldwork and detailed archival research should provide the right answer to the question about the distribution and use of land north of 'Kjølen' and in the coastal area.

Herein, four hunting complexes of differing character have been presented. The difference lies largely in their situation in the terrain. It is likely that this has also shaped both construction and hunting methods.

If one now considers the distribution of such hunting complexes for wild reindeer on Fig. 1, it will be seen that those which are discussed here cannot be representative for all resource areas. While one here exploits salt water resources, the interior of Fennoscandia is cut off from these. This will have consequences if one wishes to create a larger picture of the Saami hunting and trapping culture beyond resource exploitation and economy, and carry out comparative studies with other hunting and trapping cultures.

If one wants to draw some parallels, it must concern the hunting enclosures themselves, the principles of their construction, their placement in terrain, and so on.

In this case, when it concerns the hunting constructions for wild reindeer which have been utilized down to the last few hundred years, it is reasonable to turn to hunting cultures in the circumpolar region. It will be noted that the principle of converging enclosures and barricades has

67

been applied over the whole of Siberia, in North America, and in Greenland. Of course, pitfalls for wild reindeer have been difficult to construct on Siberian and North American tundra land. Nevertheless, pitfalls have also been employed here, although they have been designed with barriers on large snow drifts and where there has been deep snow with a hard crust layer.

But basic similarities such as these can be identified in hunting cultures in various regions throughout the world. The main point in any cultural study is clearly to discover how these principles are adapted to the available resources for the construction, the hunting object, the landscape, and the entire cultural apparatus in the various hunting societies.

Bibliography

Fellman, J.
    1906 Anteckningar, vol. IV. Helsingfors.

Hunting and Hunters in Mongolia

Bo Sommarström

The name 'Mongolia' has been chosen for this study because the main part of the material dealt with here stems from or applies to the core land of the Mongolian ethnical groups, the land that is now, politically and administratively, divided into the Mongolian People's Republic (previously called Outer Mongolia) and the Inner Mongolian Autonomous Region in the People's Republic of China (previously Inner Mongolia). There are also Mongolian populations, e.g. in the Buryat Autonomous SSR and the Tuva Autonomous Oblast in the Siberian part of the Soviet Union. Add thereto Mongolian groups in China outside the above-mentioned, vast, Inner Mongolian Region, e.g. in Kansu, Ch'ing-hai and Sinkiang, and in Afghanistan, etc.[1]

Thus, by the choice of this name, I wish to emphasize that the material available does not apply to 'all' Mongols and is not evenly distributed over all territorial divisions. This may, inter alia, be due to the fact that livestock herding is the predominant occupation among the nomads and, in addition, naturally enough more easily accessible to observation than the hunting culture, whether the latter was a complement to livestock herding or existed as a chief occupation among individuals or scattered groups.[2]

I

'Mongolia', here Outer and Inner Mongolia with adjoining territories inhabited by Mongols, is divided into very dissimilar, geographical zones: mountains and forests in the north, north-west, and north-east, and steppe, desert steppe, and true desert in the region in between; in addition, again mountains and mountainous plateaus with swamps inhabited by the groups living in the south near Tibet, on Koko Nor and Tsaidam. This means, too, that animal life is varied. Of the game suitable as food it is primarily antelope, gazelle, roedeer and deer that have been hunted on a large scale over a large part of the area, and in addi-

69

tion, quite a lot of, e.g. *wapiti* (a type of *elk*), wild yak, wild reindeer, and *argali* (wild sheep). Among furred animals, it is, above all, fox and wolf, squirrel and marmot that have been hunted, whereas bear, tiger, badger, wild camel and wild horse have had a limited importance locally. Traditionally, bird-shooting (or trapping and snaring) has been of minor importance, and then mostly pheasant, in spite of the fact that birds are abundant and of many kinds. (Fishing, too, has been inconsiderable, at some places non-existent, despite the presence of fishing-grounds.)

Hunting is pursued not only for the sake of the meat or hide/fur but also for other reasons. Elk and reindeer antler with remaining skin has been sold to Han-Chinese as aphrodisiacs, and the gall bladder of the wolf has been used by the Mongols as medicine, to give only two examples.[3]

Accounts by people who have spent long periods of time among the Mongols, e.g. M. Huc, the Catholic missionary, more than a hundred years ago, agree in considering hunting an occupation inconsiderable in relation to the stock of game. Huc says, for instance, that:

the Mongol often rides out to hunt but he always does so because he has to rather than for his own amusement, and then he does not bring his gun or bow except when he wants to kill deer, roedeer and pheasant, whereof he usually gives his king a gift. The Mongols always catch foxes on the run, since they are afraid of damaging their fur, which is highly valued among them.

Thus, they did not use snares or other kinds of traps (unlike, e.g. the Chinese) and told Huc that they preferred chasing, for 'We act fairly ...' (Huc 1862–64: 56). One type of snare was used, however, but, logically, it was attached to the end of a pole, was called *årrek,* and was chiefly used for the catching of horses, a method still employed and corresponding to the lasso of the Saamis. Huc gives a vivid account of how this pole snare was used against the wolf, which was the worst enemy of the nomads because of the havoc it wrought among their herds:

The news that a wolf has appeared in the neighbourhood is to all a signal to mount their horses and since there is always a saddled horse by every tent, the whole plain is suddenly swarming with horsemen, each of whom is armed with his long pole snare. The wolf may try to escape wherever he likes, everywhere he encounters enemies, who are charging at him, and, however inaccessible the mountain, they can pursue him, since the Mongol horses are as agile as chamois. After the horseman has got the snare around the wolf's neck, he immediately whirls around and gallops away dragging the beast after him ... (Huc 1862–64: 87).

The greatest chance to catch the wolf was, however, to find out where the antelopes were, according to the main rule that the success of hunting

Fig. 1. 'Chasseurs mongoles', drawing by Sven Hedin on his first large scientific expedition, when he travelled through Central Asia from West to East. – All pictures by courtesy of The Sven Hedin Foundation and The Ethnographical Museum of Sweden, Stockholm.

and trapping depends on a familiarity with the behaviour of the animals. Georg Söderbom, who was brought up and lived for a long time among the Mongols in Inner Mongolia, has given us this account:

At nightfall, the antelopes look for a place with tall grass where they can sleep, sheltered from the wind. Then, during the night, wolves go to lie in ambush, some along one side of the area with the tall grass, where the antelopes are, and others on the opposite side, all of them in the tall grass. And then they wait until daybreak when the antelopes begin to get up one after the other, to stretch their small legs and make their light 'wee wee' – at that moment the wolves attack and dash into the herd, half of the antelopes still being asleep. Those which are staling become paralysed where they stand, the attackers will bite savagely here and there wounding as many antelopes as possible. The main herd, of course, will rush in the direction of the ambush, and the wolves there will meet them head on, wounding as many as possible. When the main herd has disappeared, the wolves start killing and feasting. *On several occasions we have hunted a wolf just after an early morning feast*; he

71

eats so much that he can hardly run and often has to throw up his breakfast before he can start running. Many Mongolian hunters told me about this cunning of the wolf (Söderbom Ms).

II

In spite of all knowledge and hunting skill, it was still easiest to take early precautions, i.e. collect the animals, at least the cattle, sheep, and young camels, every evening and bring them to the camp. There they were herded into an enclosure or fastened to a long rope tethered to the ground. They were guarded by ferocious dogs, usually ten to fifteen in each camp, which kept the wolf at a distance.

There is a connection between hunting and war in several ways. In times of military activity, the game is driven away from their natural grounds to areas that are unguarded and not used to wolves, for instance. Then there may be great devastation, but also a large extra income for hunters. Söderbom has much material, among other things the prices of wolves' furs, from the period ca 1925–45, when he hunted much himself and organized hunting parties for others. Civil wars and wars against the Japanese had, for instance, by the middle of the 1930's, increased the havoc caused by the wolf, and the problem grew too great for the Mongolian nomads themselves, who had neither the time nor the strength to cope with it. For one single hunter, a Mongol or a Westerner, the number of wolves shot per season might then amount to 400, especially in the hard winter of 1936/37. Another reason why the Mongols have sometimes been passive hunters is, according to Owen Lattimore, that observers have prevented them simply for egotistical reasons, and have not allowed the Mongol hunter to take full responsibility for the hunt. Probably, it may be generally said, as was mentioned above, that the Mongols, like other peoples who are predominantly cattle herders, are not very interested in regular hunting, but leave that to professional individual hunters, who devote their whole or a great deal of their time to hunting and trapping (Lattimore 1930: 234 ff.).

In his comparative work on Mongolian social and kinship culture, H. H. Vreesland shows clearly, however, that there are also great regional differences between nomads. Out of his three investigated Mongolian groups, Khalkha, Chahar, and Dagor, from Outer Mongolia, south-east and east (Manchurian) Inner Mongolia, respectively, the last-mentioned turned out to be the only one to which hunting was of essential impor-

72

tance, which agrees well with the fact that the Tungus, the Manchus, and other groups within former Manchuria were always keen hunters (Vreesland 1954: 206 ff.).

Vreesland's Manchurian Mongols, the Dagor, primarily hunted pregnant cow elks, bull elks, roedeer and squirrel, thus improving their economy ,which was mainly based on domestic production. The cow elk was valued for her foetus and was hunted during the late winter (1st–3rd month in the year), when she was in an advanced stage, a *swaa*. The bull elk, *boba,* was hunted later, from the 4th to the 7th month, when his antler was like velvet, i.e. covered with skin, hard 'bark', and could be sold to the Chinese.

The roedeer, *anman,* was normally hunted from the 8th to the 10th month for its meat and hide.

The hunting grounds of the *Dagor* were the forested mountains and the tributary valleys of the River Nonni. This land was in the main ownerless, and no authority controlled it. These hunting grounds were also frequented by Manchus, Solons, Russians, and Chinese.

The hunt was organized as hunting parties for a lengthy expedition. A typical such hunting group might consist of a cart drawn by a horse and, for instance, three mounted hunters. The cart contained food, ammunition, clothes, sleeping-bags, and a light tent (against the mosquitoes, if in summer), and cooking vessels. Hunting groups were formed in two ways, one was that two hunters went out on equal terms; they had their food in common and ate together, formed 'a kettle', *neke twaa* . Either each kept his game or they pooled it all and then shared it equally, 'like luck', *neke mayin,* if they were equally good hunters. Another method was to form a partnership with others, at least one financier, who could stay at home or join the group, whichever suited him best. A hunter without any means might go to a wealthier man and ask to be equipped with, for instance, a gun, ammunition, clothes and food. This was called *anda,* which originally meant sworn, blood-brother. In return, the hunter gave him half the spoils. Then there was more occasional hunting, which occurred in the vicinity of the home village. Foxes and wolves were then hunted from horseback with the aid of hounds by individual hunters or by groups. Hawks were used to catch pheasants, partridges, and hares. Sometimes snares or traps were used to catch hares and birds.

The hunting expeditions in large groups were led by a *tatandaa, 'tent leader',* who was elected not on account of his hunting skill but because of his seniority. In winter when there was snow, the cart with the stores

Fig. 2. Resting yak and shot yak-cow, drawings by Sven Hedin.

could not be brought all the way to the hunting grounds but was left behind, and the hunters went on on horseback. Such a hiding place was not to be disturbed, except when a stranger was absolutely forced to take some of the food, and then he had to leave a mark of identification behind.

There could seldom be any poaching on these vast expanses of land and inaccessible mountains with their abundance of game. Huc gives an exception: The Imperial Forest (Huc 1862–64: 28, 31). On the other hand, customary rights and laws regarding the stealing of tools prevailed. Söderbom gives an example at great length: 'In Mongolia it is terrible to steal, and punishment for stealing is very heavy' (Söderbom 1955: 22 f.). On one occasion, his hunter had lost his antelope trap (probably a spring trap). They both saw by the tracks that an antelope had first been caught in it, and that it and the trap had been removed by somebody. They followed the tracks to a village and saw a raw antelope hide stretched out to dry, and after having searched, they also found the proof of the theft, the trap itself. A fifteen-year-old boy turned out to be the culprit. Söderbom wanted to leave the matter alone if only the boy's father taught him a lesson, but somehow the matter leaked out immediately. Messengers came riding from the local man in authority, a prince, and within a week the thief had been convicted. For half a year he had to work at gathering fuel, dry camel dung, and transporting food to the local administration. In between, he sat with a wooden collar around his neck in a cage-like tent contraption without the felt tent cloths, so that everyone could see him clearly. However, he slept in an ordinary tent at nights and was not harshly treated.

Nowadays nature conservation prevails in Mongolia, and there are detailed game-protection laws: We can refer to the law that has been in force since 1953 for the Mongolian People's Republic (Schubert 1971: 215 ff.): the hunting of 19 animals is prohibited, e.g. marten, wild reindeer, nightingale, etc., and close seasons are prescribed for marmot, wild boar, brown roedeer, antelope, gazelle, etc. In a companion work to the law dealing with the stock of animals in the Republic there is also a description of catching methods for birds: net traps (*tor*), cage traps (*xunz*), snares (*urxi*), etc. Locally, there still occurs hunting with eagles, which can even kill wolves.

III

The permanent or temporary close seasons for certain areas may be called an older type of nature conservation. They apply particularly to the mountain peaks and temples that were determined by the Lamaist authorities or were at least codified by them. Here, too, we quote an example from Georg Söderbom, who often encountered such places (Söderbom Ms):

In the protected hills where the Mongol fear hunting may offend the Lord Spirit of the Mountain, or the Gacherin Echin, the Lord Spirit of the Earth, one can as a rule recognize such hills by the cairn or *Obo* that crowns the dominating peak of the sacred mountain. In such hills, I have chased argali on foot, they just look at you foolishly, run a little and sneeze a little then look at you again ... Naturally one has to be very careful not to get caught hunting in these protected areas, however there is always a way to get around these restrictions, if you know how and do not get caught by the lamas or the particularly religious laymen, it's alright, but you must conform with the customs, after shooting a sheep you take off the head itself and lay it against a rock that vaguely resembles a sheep's body, lying down, so that when the Lord Spirit of the Mountain comes out to count his sheep and finds one missing he will be deceived and will from afar off see it lying down, resting or sleeping, and so he will be satisfied. For a Mongol this may be alright as he is not interested in the horns, but for the westerner who is out specifically to bring back the horns as trophies he will never want to leave the horns behind.

These close seasons could sometimes be related to certain events, for instance once in 1931, when a prohibition was proclaimed by Panchen Lama against the hunting of antelope in the Sunit region, eastern Inner Mongolia. In all probability, the reason was that some person of high rank had died and was expected to be re-incarnated as an antelope (Montell 1934: 112).

The general attitude of Buddhism to animals is also reflected in many cases where this religion has incorporated ancient conceptions and customs with regard to animals. Among other things, we may mention the *prohibition* for a believer against *killing.* Much has been written about it, but its origin has hardly been clarified. The most important symbol is, perhaps, for the façades of the Lamaist temples to be decorated with a gilt bronze group with Dharma chakra, the Wheel of Knowledge, in the centre, flanked by two deer. The latter, heraldic, animals are to remind us of the princely background of Buddha Gautama, and the fact that he renounced the world for the sake of Faith and Enlightenment. The prohibition against killing is, in reality, evaded in subtle ways; when people are concerned, e.g., a *khattak,* gift shawl, is 'made' to commit the deed for you, and when it is a question of animals, you eat animals that 'other', special people have slaughtered and consequently have to be regarded as pariah.

Walter Bosshard once asked his Mongol companion on his journeys,

76

Fig. 3. Heads of wild (to the left) and tame camel, drawn by Sven Hedin.

the Lama Arasj, who had participated in a hunt: 'Does your religion not forbid you to kill animals?' Arasj answered: 'The Gods know that these beasts of prey attack our herds. Which is better, one wolf or ten sheep? At any rate, during the next few days we are going to sacrifice a bowl of rice and a lot of meat to the Gods. Then they cannot become incensed with us for the sake of two grown-up wolves and four cubs' (Bosshard 1938: 116).

Among Tibetans in the Indian Himalayas, I have seen game, such as, for instance, deer and fox, which have been put on the walls in public buildings and have been provided with a white *khattak* (at Dharamsala and Rajpur).

Generally speaking, the fox has not an exceptional position in «Mongolia» compared with other animals. It is, however, considered unlucky by hunters to encounter a fox by accident at the beginning of a hunt, and there are many who then even break off the hunt. In the north, among the Buryat, the fox is associated with the lower regions, as the dog of Erlig Khan (cf. the four-eyed dog, and Stallo and the wolf/dog among the Saamis, and the Scandinavian fox-tailed wood-spirits). In the south among the Ordos Mongols, people talk about transformations of fox spirits and fox women, which probably stem from the Chinese, like the Japanese female fox figures Dakini-ten (Heissig 1976: 475).

Still, the fox plays an interesting role in one particular context among the Mongols in various parts of 'Mongolia'. In later years, a number of articles have been published in *Zentralasiatische Studien* on *fox sacrifice texts (Ünegen-ü sang)* in different versions, by the Mongolists H. Serruys, C. R. Bawden, and W. Heissig. 'The-Sacrifice-of-the-Fox' ritual is, in a syncretistic form, chiefly a ritual for originally real animals of sacrifice, popular-religious with a thin veneer of Buddhist terminology and conceptions of faith. The sacrifice is nowaday mostly made with incense but, according to information received, it has also been made with sugar, fruit, flower, butter, jewels. It is a ceremony purifying all kinds of sins and 'impurities', which is characteristic of Buddhism (Bawden 1976: 440 f., 1978: 9, 10, 12). Now for *some lines out of this fox sacrifice text* (Serruys 1970: 318 f.):

During a period of early times (Garudi) with the title of King of Birds united with his companions, mixed sin and uncleanness and nine foxes were born; and so all sin and uncleanness went out. [Hey!] The people of that time caught the foxes and using various means, killed them and made them into an offering.

Hey! For uncleanness of powerful Heaven we worship with their heads. For uncleanness of the Sun and the Moon we worship with their eyes. For uncleanness of the dakinis we worship with their noses. For uncleanness of the lightning we worship with their tongues. For (uncleanness of) the Four Most Powerful, we worship with their legs. For uncleanness of the Angry Deity we worship with their hearts. For uncleanness of the Snowy Mountains we worship with their lungs. For uncleanness of the *Bitege-kitegen* we worship with their livers. For uncleanness of the lakes we worship with their stomachs. For uncleanness of the seas we worship with their necks. For uncleanness of the rocks we worship with their bones. For uncleanness of the land and places we worship with their flesh. For uncleanness of sources and waters we worship with their blood. For *güdün* and uncleanness of woods and forests we worship with their hair. The sea of the lower level we worship with their joints. The places of direction of neighbours we worship with their spine. The guardian of the day and the night we worship with their ribs. [For all impurities we worship with their bodies.]

Heissig associates some parts of the fox incense offering with ancient animal sacrifices entailing the putting out of the separate parts of the body, proved to take place among the Mongols as far as elk and bear are concerned. He considers, too, that the detailed accounts of all the characteristics of the fox bear witness to the great age of the ritual, and that they partly correspond to otherwise common substitute and taboo designations among Mongol hunters (Heissig 1976: 488). On the other hand, he believes that the content of the legend reflects quite late Indian models in Purañas, especially the enmity between the bird Garuda and

Nāgas, the snakes. He concludes: 'Die . . . Vielschichtigkeit der "Fuchs-Opfer"-Texte gibt ein Musterbeispiel für die Synkretistische Inkorporationsmethodik das PopulärBuddhismus gegenüber der Volksreligion der Mongolei', and he ends by saying that it takes much work to sift the pre-Buddhist parts in Mongol literature and folklore (Heissig 1976: 493 f.).

IV

To this interdisciplinary future programme one would wish to add that much could probably be gained if one were to add ethnographical and historical studies with *an anthropological orientation and an ecological outlook.*

For instance, there probably remains much to be done for the further analysis of the animal dance masks in the Lamaist mystery-play ritual *Cham.* Take, for instance, the Deer mask (Tib. *Śa-'bar*), which embodies the Wind God or his equine animals. The Wind God, whose pictures on the prayer flags are seen everywhere in mountain passes at temples and river-crossings, protects the north-western heavenly direction (from which, incidentally, the predominant wind comes in Mongolia).

Moreover, compare the fox sacrifice ritual with the practice in Bronze Age China, where hunting cult feasts were celebrated with the sacrifice of game, and where during the Chou dynasty ceremonial archery was pursued as a combination of a feudal sport and a religious 'meditative' training: they shot at a target consisting of the animals of the Zodiac, and they measured the distance to it with a special 'fox step measure', and sang the 'song of the fox head' (Eberhard 1942 a: Reihe 3, Reihe 8; cf. the dance of the Mongol and the Bhutanese to the glory of Buddha after a victory in archery!).

Compare, for the same period of time, the Bronze Age and the Early Iron Age, the Euro-Asian *animal style* among Scythians, Huns and other steppe peoples. Let us quote Karl Jettmar:

Der Unterschied zwischen Jägern und modernen Nomaden liesse sich psychologisch erklären: Die heute zur Sesshaftigkeit übergehenden Nomadenvölker der Steppe hatten trotz aller Liebe des Reiters zu seinen Pferd nicht das gleiche, sich zu fast sexueller Spanning steigernde Verhältnis zum Tier (Jettmar 1964: 11).

He states that the oldest steppe animal style originated with hunting peoples from the Taiga in the north, i.a. because it portrays very reindeer-like deer. Jettmar ends his account of this animal style art by referring

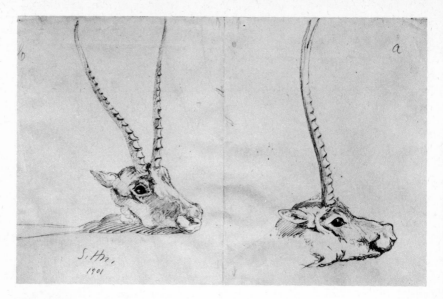

Fig. 4. Two buck-heads of antelope, drawn by Sven Hedin.

to the fact that Genghis Khan is considered to be the offspring of a wolf and a hind, according to the secret Mongolian Chronicle, and that his name, Temuchin, means smith (Jettmar 1964: 242).

With Owen Lattimore (Lattimore 1940: 161 ff.) and Johan Gunnar Andersson (1929) we may go still further back in time and discuss the emergence of domesticated animals and then touch upon oasis/desert/agriculture relations. We may analyse the animals on the numerous Mongolian and other Central-Asian and North-Asian rock-carvings, among which have recently been found 'tied camels' reproduced '3000 years ago'.

But to satisfy such ambitions and programmes demands, among other things, an intensified source criticism and a systematic analysis of written sources as, for instance, Chang Kwang-Chih has done in his new classification of Shang and Chou myths in articles in the Bulletin of the Institute of Ethnology, *Academia Sinica* (from No. 14, 1962). There we may have use for a renewed analysis of data about the technology of hunting, as in W. Böttger's 'Die ursprünglichen Jagdmethoden der Chinesen' (1960) but keeping, at the same time, a watchful eye on the archaeological find results of recent years, in China and in 'Mongolia'.

But we should not only deal with ancient history. If we keep only to the period between the two world wars, there is much interesting material in, among other places, the Ethnographical Museum of Stockholm, which sheds light on hunting as part of trade economy and, thereby, also on the political development.

Generally speaking, it is often difficult to obtain sufficient concrete information about the technology of hunting (the construction of traps, for instance) and its methods (arrangements of the tools such as, for instance low traps and hunting pit systems), the organization of hunting groups and the distribution of the spoils through trade, tribute, and domestic production, i.e. economic anthropology, and conceptions of faith and rituals. Here, we have to go through cameral archives, local and central laws and statutes, and district chronicles ('gazetteers') from, above all, China. Differences between Mongol groups – e.g. in Vreesland between his three types of societies, or in Eberhard between his disparate 'ancient Mongol' – may partly disappear or be replaced by others.

In any case, the picture will become deeper, the reflection of the relationship between animal and man, where hunting is only one aspect of the issue. One way of regarding that relationship is that of the Bhuddhists, where in *Bhaga chakra,* The 'Wheel of Life', of the six 'Worlds' one is for man, another for animals, and where one lands in the cycle of reincarnation depends on one's behaviour. The question is whether this philosophy has essentially influenced the hunting of the Mongol, or if it simply suited the attitude that was already there.

Notes

1 For general backgrounds and maps, see e.g. the surveys of Ferdinand 1968, Herrmann 1935, König 1967 and The Times Atlas of China 1973–1974.
2 The present study was inspired by a draft MS written by Georg Söderbom and given to the Sven Hedin Foundation at the Ethnographical Museum of Sweden in Stockholm, after his death (in 1973). Some of the information there had been used by Söderbom himself in the two publications mentioned under his name in the reference list. He also had a lot of stories from his own experience as a hunter of wolves, deer, and *argali* sheep, which he had planned to publish, and part of which has been tape-recorded by friends. Söderbom was also adviser and informant to Gösta Montell and other members of the Sino-Swedish Expedition 1927–35, and some of his knowledge of local life amongst the nomads and Han-Chinese border population was used in their reports.
3 Söderbom's MS, *inter alia* in both of the two drafts on hunting, and from a third MS in his collection.

Bibliography

Andersson, J. G.
1929 Der Weg über den Steppen. Bulletin of the Museum of Far Eastern Antiquities, Vol. 1. Stockholm.
Bawden, Ch. R.
1976 The 'Offering of the Fox' again. Zentralasiatische Studien 10. Wiesbaden.
1978 An Oirat Manuscript of the 'Offering of the Fox'. Zentralasiatische Studien 12. Wiesbaden.
Bosshard, W.
1938 Kühles Grasland Mongolei. Berlin.
Böttger, W.
1960 Die ursprünglichen Jagdmethoden der Chinesen. Berlin.
Chang, K.-Ch.
1962 A Classification of Shang and Chou Myths. Bulletin of the Institute of Ethnology, Academia Sinica, Vol. 14. Taipei.
Eberhard, W.
1942 a Kultur und Siedlung der Randvölker Chinas. Leiden.
1942 b Lokalkulturen im alten China. Leiden.
Ferdinand, K.
1968 Centralasien, in: Verdens folkeslag i vor tid, ed. by G. Nellemann and J. Nicolaisen. Copenhagen.
Haslund-Christensen, H.
1933 Jabonah: Pionjärliv i Mongoliet. Stockholm.
Heaton, W.
1976 Inner Mongolia: The Haos and Huais of Chinese Policy toward the Mongols. Mongolian Studies, Journal of the Mongolia Society, Vol. 3. Bloomington.
Hedin, S.
1926 My Life as an Explorer. London.
Heissig, W.
1964 Ein Volk sucht seine Geschichte. Düsseldorf/Wien.
1976 Zur Morphologie der 'Fuchsopfer'-Gebete. Zentralasiatische Studien 10. Wiesbaden.
Herrmann, A.
1935 Historical and Commercial Atlas of China. Cambridge, Mass.
Huc, E. R.
1862–64 Souvenirs d'un voyage dans la Tartarie, le Thibet et la Chine pendant les années 1844, 1845 et 1846. Swedish translation from original edition (Paris 1850). Stockholm.
Jettmar, K.
1964 Die frühen Steppenvölker. Kunst der Welt. Baden-Baden.
König, W.
1967 Mongolei. Erläuterungen zu einer Ausstellung im Museum für Völkerkunde Leipzig. Leipzig.
Kozlow, P. K.
1925 Mongolei, Amdo und die tote Stadt Chara-Choto. Die Expedition der Russischen Geographischen Gesellschaft 1907–09. German translation from Russian original. Berlin.
Lattimore, O.
1933 High Tartary. Boston.
1940 Inner Asian Frontiers of China. New York.

'Mongolia'
    1976 'Mongolia', booklet published by The Diplomatist Publications Ltd., London.

Montell, G.
    1934 Våra vänner på stäppen. Genom Mongoliet till torgoterna vid Etsingol. Stockholm.

Norrmann, K. E. and H. Engman
    1969 Mongoliet. Den första folkrepubliken. Stockholm.

Schubert, J.
    1971 Paralipomena Mongolica. Wissenschaftliche Notizen über Land, Leute und Lebensweise in der Mongolischen Volksrepublik. Berlin.

Serruys, H.
    1970 Offering of the Fox: A Shamanist Text from Ordos. Zentralasiatische Studien 4. Wiesbaden.

Söderbom, G.
    1954 Bortom kinesiska muren. Skildringar från Mongoliet (together with E. Söderbom). Stockholm.
    1955 Inner Mongolia. Mimeographed draft, 'Annex A, Basic Background Information prepared for WAHRAF, U.S.A.' Archives of the Ethnographical Museum of Sweden.
    Ms Hunting in Mongolia. Archives of the Ethnographical Museum of Sweden.

The Times Atlas of China
    1973–74 The Minority Peoples, pp. XVIII–XIX. Tokyo and London.

Vreesland, H.
    1954 Mongol Community and Kinship Structure. Behavior Science Monographs, Human Relations Area Files. New Haven.

II
Hunting Economy

Aspects of hunting economy are found in several of the articles published in this volume, for obvious reasons: the whole existence of the hunter revolves around the consumption or barter and sale of the hunted game, unless – and this is an important reservation – hunting occupies a less important niche in a more complex society. There is, indeed, a far step between the Eskimo or Australian huntsman whose entire life is dependent upon the catches he can make and the animals he can kill and the feudal aristocratic lord in Europe who hunts for pleasure, tradition, and social status.

The following paper by Phebe Fjellström illuminates the exchange in trade and taxes between the Saamis and the Scandinavian authorities during Mediaeval times. It shows the ways in which a hunting economy functions within the framework of a dominant state society, and illustrates articles of trade and their use. The main value of the paper lies in the fact that it discloses economic patterns from a remote age.

Northern Scandinavian Hunting Culture as Reflected in Mediaeval Records

Phebe Fjellström

For several hundred years, the Saamis have supplied pelts, fish and fowl to the greater part of Scandinavia and Western Europe. When, in 1946, Nils Ahnlund wrote his article *Norlandish Pelt Taxes,* he stated that a study '. . . of Crown purchases of pelts extending over the greater part of Norrland . . . could well deserve to be investigated' and that 'the subject has not yet been studied in its entirety'. (Ahnlund, 1946: 44.) He did not take this up, nor did he analyse the Saamis' pelt trade on the basis of the pelt-taxes which are described in detail in the records from the 16th and 17th centuries in Swedish Lappland. Instead he deals mainly with the registers of pelt taxes from Norrland, i.e. from the records concerning *Dalarna, Helsingland* and *Ångermanland,* as the title of his article suggests.[1] Åke Hultkrantz has, however, in an early ethnological essay, dealt with this matter. The essay is unpublished, but is mentioned by Ahnlund.[2]

In the dissertation *Lappish Silver* (Fjellström, 1962) attention was paid for the first time to Northern Swedish purchases of pelts, with particular attention being given to the respective roles of the Crown and the Saamis. In order to give an over-view of the diversity of the trade and taxation systems that existed in Northern Sweden, with its pelt revenues and pelt trade, and, most especially, its special clearing system for the exchange of goods, the dissertation presented lists of goods showing the variety of goods in all Saami territories during a certain period of time, and also the amount of goods in circulation at the particular time.

The tables are built upon detailed study of 16th and 17th century records of pelt and silver taxation rolls from *Ume* and *Ångermanland* Saami districts, together with those of *Pite, Lule, Torne, Kemi* and *Varanger.* It is nevertheless justifiable to study these tables again, but from another viewpoint. According to the tables for Lappish Silver, during the period 1555–1560 a quantity of 2090 'squirrel' (squirrel pelts = *gråverk*) were disposed of from the Saami area of *Torne*; from *Lule*, 1155 pelts, from *Pite*, 474 pelts, and from *Umeå* and *Ångermanland* Saami areas, 4080 squirrel pelts. (See fig. I, p 14; Fjellström, 1962, I: 301.) The tables even show that apart from reindeer and elk skins, there was a contemporary circulation of the skins of ermine, wolverine, marten, fox, wolf, bear and otter in Lappish trade. Beaver pelts were, however, somewhat rare.[3]

Two centuries later, in 1747, Pehr Högström wrote about the lively Lappish trade in *Beskrifning öfwer de til Sweriges krona lydande lapmarker* (Description of the Lapp areas subject to the Swedish Crown), p. 246. In his book, he makes particular reference to trade and to pelts and lists, among other things, the types of pelts which correspond to those in our tables.

A century later still, in the 19th century, J. A. Nensén provided, in his collection of hand-written material, information concerning types of pelts and hunting catches from the Saami areas of Northern Sweden which also correspond to the tables. In other words, there was a basically similar assortment of pelts in circulation from the 16th century to the middle of the 19th century. Even prior to the 16th century, the same continuity of pelt catches can be traced in Northern Scandinavia.

This claim is supported by records from, among others, English and German areas, records which appear to reflect indirectly the hunting pattern of Northern Scandinavia. These sources contain research material which has, as yet, not been examined. A close cooperation between philologists and ethnologists based on this material would certainly be productive. In the rest of this article, purely ethnological problem frameworks are examined.

Problem Framework and Method

Particular points of interest in connection with the examination of mediaeval source material are here:

1 The extent to which the source material provides information concerning which ethnic groups were involved in pelt trading. Is it possible to trace the role of the Saamis in this?
2 If the Northern Scandinavian hunting catch – in this case, pelt catches – remained the same from the mediaeval period throughout the 16th century and on to the 20th century, should not the hunting pattern, that is, instruments of hunting and hunting methods, have remained of a similar nature?

The latter question can only be briefly taken up for discussion here.

Nevertheless, the material which concerns this area of study has been collated for subsequent publication in a work on *Saami Society – Tradition and Present*. In order to answer the question of the continuity of the hunting pattern during almost 700 years, not only older records must be used, but also more recent ethnographic material . Material gathered during field-work in our own century must be used. Recordings and interviews made recently concerning hunting and trapping are especially useful when placed in a macroperspective.

Working with 14th century material, on the one hand, and with recordings made in the 1960's on the other is by no means unusual for today's ethnologist. We oscillate between the deep perspective of written sources = the historical aspect and the close view = the social view – gathered on the individual level. Informers in the field can still give a sudden illuminating picture of a bygone time, and link us to the present. This is most especially true of field-work in the Northern Swedish area – one of the few areas of industrialized Western Europe which still offer that opportunity.

With the help of mediaeval records, a summarized picture of those pelts that were in circulation during the Middle Ages and which come from northenmost Europe will be presented. It is also meaningful in this context to seek to trace the active role played by the Saamis. We know that they acquired pelts, that they hunted and fully mastered the hunting culture of Northern Scandinavia, and this already during the Middle Ages. They were, however, in no way alone in possessing these skills. The hunting culture within the area of Northern Eurasia was widespread, not least in prehistoric times – without a knowledge of hunting and trapping, the inhabitants of *Ärjemark* (the wilderness = *ɦ:erämaa*) could not have survived. The hunting pattern was here, as in other areas of the world, conditioned to the ecological situation, that is to say that forms and methods of hunting and trapping were totally assimilated into the total environment in order to achieve maximum results. That which we today would call 'typically Saami hunting methods' is probably a reflection of a hunting culture that formerly existed throughout the entire Northern Eurasian area.

For the ethnologist it is from a methodological viewpoint quite natural to examine consistencies and inconsistencies in material, that is to eliminate cultural variables against the background of the ecological environment. Such cultural variables are quite reliable: for example, between Saamis and settlers, between Norwegian Finmark and Northern Russia, etc.

*

We shall now move on to examine the mediaeval material. I have used four sources.

1. *Norges gamle love* indtil 1387, Vol. 1–5, 1846–1895. Ed. by R. Keyser and P. A. Munch, (Vol. 5) Gustaf Storm and Ebbe Hertzberg. (NGL)
2. *Diplomatarium Norwegicum,* Vol. 19. Ed. by Alexander Bugge, Kria, 1910. (DN)
3. *Hansische Urkundenbücher.* Ed. by K. Höhlbaum and Karl Kunze.
4. *Mecklenburgisches Urkundenbuch,* Vol. 22 (1907).

The informative mediaeval Customs records which are to be found in the Public Records office in London, and in the British Museum, and which have been collected by Alexander Bugge, are concerned with trade between Norway, England, Gotland, and the Hansa cities. They are printed in DN 19, and are of the greatest value in getting an estimation of North European pelt trade at the beginning of the 14th century. As long ago as in 1898, Bugge analyzed the material in his article *Handelen mellem England og Norge indtil begyndelsen af det 15de aarhundrede* (Trade between England and Norway up to the Beginning of the 15th Century) (Bugge 1898; see also Bugge 1898/99, 1899).

Bugge analyzes, among other things, the assortment of goods, and directs his attention primarily to the important Norwegian export articles, namely fish, and thus interprets certain lists of goods which were unclear. In the English Customs material, there are lists in Latin, Low German, and probably dialect. The Hanseatic material consists primarily of lists in Low German, but also lists in Latin, and in certain dialects which are difficult to interpret, and which, in some cases, are as yet uninvestigated. To this we shall return. Bugge even interested himself in Norwegian timber exports, and, on a lesser scale, strangely enough, in the export of pelts. He draws up a list in which he translates and explains the names of goods from Latin and Low German (Bugge, 1899: 219). In 1914, B. E. Bendixen wrote a critical article entitled *Vareomsætningen mellem England og Norge i første halvdel av 14 aarhundrede* (Trade Turnover between England and Norway during the First Half of the 14th Century) (pp 277–313, 444–471), in which he examined Bugge's presentation. Even Bendixen takes up the matter of pelts, but very briefly. Consequently there exists a particular aspect of hunting – pelt catches – which is almost unexamined in this mediaeval source material. It can indirectly provide us with a picture of the hunting culture and the social life of the northenmost areas of Europe during the 14th century.

Correctly interpreted and evaluated, it can point towards a clearer understanding of hunting methods, animal life, clothing habits, and towards an understanding of life styles in Northern Eurasia.

*

On the basis of the tables of goods, which in turn are based on Northern Scandinavian records from the 16th century (Fjellström, 1962, I: 228), we can draw up the hypothesis that the respective pelt types contained in the tables appear in similar proportions even during the 14th and 15th centuries. If that be the case, squirrel pelts ought to have been mentioned more often in mediaeval source material and to have existed in large quantities. We shall first examine the English Customs records. As expected, we find between the 4th July and the 29th September 1304 repeated cases of squirrel pelts (*griseum opere*) being examined by Customs authorities at Hull and Ravensworth. (*Griseum opere* were the most valuable of squirrel pelts.) Thus 'griseo opere valoris 20 li. – griseo opere valoris 67 li. – griseo opere valoris 68 li. – griseo opere valoris 36 li. – griseo opere valoris 416 li.' (DN 19: 489).

Between the 5th February 1303 and the 26th June 1304 in Lynn, a large number of Norwegian ships passed through Customs. Among the goods was noted 'grisio opere valoris 20 libr.' (DN 19: 465). Mention is also made in the Customs lists of 'Roskin' (DN: 475), 'Redwerk' (DN: 474), or '50 tymbre de Rosykin' (50 timmer = 2000 pelts, red pelts). 'Roskin' and 'redwerk' mean 'red pelt' and refer, according to Bugge, to the skin of the red squirrel, which, according to Schiller-Lübben's *Mittelniederdeutsches Wörterbuch* (1877, Vol. 3) is rôtwerk = rothes Pelzwerk; in other words, he includes red skins from other creatures, for example the red fox (Bugge, 1899: 219; Bendixen, 1914–1916: 452). Squirrel pelts are found in varying qualities and forms. They must have been extremely fashionable for clothing throughout Europe, since they were delivered in enormous quantities from not merely the polar region, but also from the Baltic area, from Northern Russia, and even from Småland! In the records from Meckelburg (*Mecklenburgisches Urkundenbuch* 22: 293) mention is made of a ship which was hijacked in 1393 while *en route* from Wismar to Lübeck. Among the goods that were reported lost were: 87 timmer operis (squirrel pelts), 2 timmer ermine, 3 timmer 'Smolensekeswerkes' (that is, red squirrel pelts from Småland), 1 timmer 'rodes Littowescheswerkes' (red squirrel pelts from Lithuania).

In order to gain an idea of the wide variation in nomenclature concerning squirrel pelts, it is necessary to know a little of the various species of squirrel, and the various pelt qualities. I shall allow an informant to speak. The recording was made in 1956.

Amon Jonsson, from the parish of Stensele, the village of Slussfors, was born in 1886. He explains how squirrels were not allowed to be shot before they were 'gill', that is, before their coats were fully grown. If they were shot before they were 'gill', it would be apparent from the flayed pelt, which, when it was 'snodd' (twisted off) would show a blue stripe up the back (also known as a 'blåbakarn' or 'blue-back'). (*Dialekt- och ortnamnsarkivet*, DAUM, Umeå: Gr 525 A, Olof Grönlund, Granliden, Vilhelmina.) 'When the squirrel was "gill", it was so white and nice', when the pelt was flayed. As late as 5th November, the squirrel 'could be blue in the back'. In that case, one only received one-third of the going price. These pelts were regarded as sub-standard, and were used as fur lining in the arms. The informant Grönlund also relates that there used to be large numbers of 'grey squirrel, and *"tallikorn"*, the red one, and *"polarikorn"* in the mountain forest, but now only the grey'. (Grönlund, born 1879, DAUM: Gr 525.) The above-named English Customs listings of 'gråverk', the 14th century 'pelles de Grayskin' are equivalent to the *'granikorn'*. It is possible that 'roytskin' (see above) is also the same as *'tallikorn'* with its red-brown fur. August Berglund from Krokträsk, born 1877, (DAUM, Gr 298 B) explains that around 1920 'there were plenty of squirrels', that they were shot up in the trees using 'blunderbusses, Huskvarnas'. The squirrel pelts were sold in Älvsbyn, and the going price was '1:50, 1:75 and 2:50 per pelt' (Swedish crowns), "the best ones were the grey". One could shoot squirrels at *Andersmas,* one month before Christmas, and then they were at their best – light grey. It was easy to flay a squirrel. 'Using the thumb, one flayed from the head over and down and clipped off the pelt at the rump.'

The squirrel pelts, *griseum opere* or *pelles de Grayskin,* mentioned above in Customs list, ought therefore to be comparable to these tree squirrels, but also to the polar squirrel. It is also probable that 'roytskin' and 'redwerk' refer to the red squirrel – the pine squirrel that was common in Småland, among other areas. However, traders at that time appear not to have used the squirrel pelt in its entirety, but to have cut off the best parts and sold them separately. The best parts of the pelt were the back and the head. Even the squirrel tails appear to have been sold separately. Are these claims reflected in the mediaeval source material? Let us see! In the Wismar Inventory drawn up between 1438 and 1547 it is stated (Schiller–Lübben Vol. 3): 'Dit sint Joh, de(s)buntmakers nagelaten guder, tom ersten I woder roetwerk, I woder nachken, I woder buntwerk, it II *tymmer bruner rygghe grawerk'*. In other words, Johannes the furrier left goods comprising 1 foder (roughly one small wagonload) of red pelts, that is, red squirrel pelts, presumably pine squirrel pelts and possibly some fox, 1 foder of 'heads' (about which, more later), 1 foder of 'buntwerk' comprising broken pelts, and finally *2 timmer (= 80) shining squirrel back pelts*. The white belly and head sections of the pelt were considered to be of less desirable quality, and were used as lining for furs, in arms, in hoods, etc. If these sections were cut off and sold separately, then they ought to have had a specific name. What do the mediaeval sources say? In my opinion, the term *buntwerk* or bundles, refers to these sections of squirrel belly, grey pelt, red pelt, all from the squirrel, but even less desirable sections of fox fur, and marten fur might be included. *Buntwerk* ought to mean 'miscellaneous' or 'various types of pelt'. The furrier was acquainted with all of these various types of fur, and used them all in his craft. As support for my claim, I should cite Schiller-Lübben, who states (Vol. 3: 523) 'Das Rückenfell (der Eichhörnchen). Die Bauchfelle heissen bunt.'

That the squirrel pelt was one of the most important articles of trade may be seen partly from the tables in Figure 1, and partly from specific expressions in the Lappish language. In Southern Lappish there is the term *årrew arto,* meaning 10 squirrel pelts. In other words, the expression reflects the mediaeval customs term *dacre* (= 10) *griseo opere* (arto = 10). *Årre* means squirrel, but it also means 'money'. (Lindahl-Öhrling, 1780: 578); *Akt årrats* = allenast en styfver (only one cent) (Grundström 1946–1954: 1512). As late as 1780, a special trading expression was thus still in circulation which bears witness to the lively trade in squirrel pelts among the Lapps during the Middle Ages and down through subsequent centuries. Another expression should also be noted – one which has never been referred to in the relevant literature – that cargo arriving in Kingston-upon-Hull between 1382–83 comprised, apart from various Norwegian goods such as *piscibus* (fish), *3 dacr pellium caprarum* (30 sheepskins), *2 barellis Whalspike* (whale blubber), *24 ereskyns* (DN 19: 273). Nobody has been able to decipher this presumably dialect term. To a Lappologist with knowledge of the Saami part in the fur trade, it seems natural to translate the term as coming from *årre,* that is to say, squirrel pelts. It can in any case not refer to either marten, fox, polecat or ermine – there are specific terms for these types of pelt. Marten is not unknown in this context, particularly in Hanseatic source material, where it is referred to as *marten* or *maerten*. In my opinion, the export of marten pelts from Northern Scandinavia

LISTS OF GOODS
(Gråverk = squirrels)

1555–1561	Torne lappmark	Lule lappmark	Pite lappmark	Ume och Angermansland lappmark
Silver[1]	428 lod	63,5 lod	32,5 lod	
Daler[1]	93½	14	1	
Penningar[1]	878	129	29	
Kittlar	7			
Gammal mässing	3 lisp.			
Tennkannor	4			
Koppar (kitlar)	12			
Kläde[2]	1132 alnar			
Vadmäl				242 alnar
Lappeskor	21	11 par	12 par	
Märd	194	193	251	1668
Gråverk	2190	1155	474	4080
Järv	36	23	21	11
Varg	24	17	13	5
Utter	20		2	
Björn	6	1	5	13
Lo				
Hermelin	54	338	105	34
Bäver	26		8	14
Svarträv	27	28	10	2
Korsräv	30	4	22	40
Fjällracka	56	38		
Renhudar	106		72	10
Älghudar				42
Renar[3]	653	236	120	73
Gäddor	10 lisp.	3 skipp. 6 lisp.	6 skipp. 17 lisp.	12 lisp.
Benlöse gäddor		2½ skipp.		23 skipp. 18½ lisp.
Finske gäddor				9 skipp.
Lappe gäddor		11 lisp.	1 skipp. 13 lisp.	
Strenge-lax	5 lisp.[4]	10 lisp.		
Bernfisk	5 skipp. 9½ lisp.		1 skipp.	
Röding		13½ lisp.	2 lisp.	
Harr		14 lisp		
Abborre		6 lisp.	3 skipp. 8 lisp.	
Sik	11 skipp. 7 lisp.	3 skipp. 14 lisp.	2 skipp.	

[1] Skatte- och saköres.
[2] Engelsk, nerisk, brabantsk, foderduk.
[3] Inventarium.
[4] Från Kemi lpmk.

was less common than the export of squirrel pelts and 'bundles'. On the other hand, marten pelts were extremely common trade goods from the Baltic and Russian areas. There are references in Hanseatic source material, for example, to 'de maerter voder – 39 maerten' (one cartload of marten pelts – 39 pelts – Schiller-Lübben, op.cit. 3, p. 39).

In *Norges gamle love* (Vol. 3, No 120, p. 221) can be found included in King Olaf Haakonssøn's law roll, an excise list for craftsmen in market towns and for country markets, describing, among other things, the pelts which were taxed during 1384, in a document which comprises a number of interesting items of information. For example, mention is made of *lambaskinnom af reine,* the skins of reindeer calves. However, there is a footnote to the effect that two copies of the original document have formed the basis of *Norges gamle love.* The first copy contains the comment 'have read reindeer, but not investigated the word' from the publisher. It is therefore not clear to what extent the skins of reindeer calves formed part of trade at that time. In my opinion, the skins of reindeer calves and ordinary reindeer skins formed an important part of mediaeval trade – we have merely not been receptive – pre-programmed – to the idea. But the proof is certainly there. If we turn to the English Customs material, we find that between 1305 and 1306 there arrived in Kingston-upon-Hull and Ravensworth from Norway 'Ij dacre de Reynder precij – 8 shilling' (DN 19: 535), '6 dacre pellium de Reynder precij – 16 shilling' (DN 19: 536), '1 dacre pellium de Reynder precij – 8 shilling' (DN 19: 540), '2 tymber de Reynder precij – 8 sh' (DN 19: 534). In fact, not a large quantity of skins, only 170 in all. What is referred to here is presumably reindeer skin with hair left on, *pellium* suggests this. Such skins can hardly have been desirable other than as undercovers for beds, or as floor coverings – in other words, as warmth-giving material. In clothes, it was not this type of skin that was in use on the Continent, and neither was it in the damp British climate. What, on the other hand, should have been a most desirable article of Saami export would have been the chamois or tanned reindeer skin – with the hair removed and tanned with fat or with alderbark. Chamois-type skins were delivered to the Royal Tannery in Stockholm, according to the National Archive (Fjellström, 1962 I: 268). No researcher has mentioned this possibility. On the other hand, some have pitted their wits against the lists of goods which are common in mediaeval source material. For example: When Duke Albrecht of Bavaria, the Dutch Regent, gave his merchants royal permission to engage in free trade from the North Sea and included the whole of the Holy Roman Empire, the goods concerned were listed. The goods are listed in regional categories. Goods from the Orient 'saffran, ginger, pepper, cinnamon, nutmeg, etc' are listed in one group, while those goods that clearly come from northernmost Europe are listed separately. Thus: 'scone werc, roet werc, zwart werc, scevenesse, hasenballinghe, hermalin, lasten, twee scellinge, ses penn Holl'

(*Hansisches Urkundenbuch*, Vol. 4: 41). The permission was given for the period 1361–1392. The word 'schevenesse' (even spelled 'scheuenisse', in the *Hansisches Urkundenbuch*) has been described by Karl Kunze in his Register (Vol. 4, p. 519) as 'eigentlich ein Sack aus Eichhörnchenfellen', and in the *Meckelburgsches Urkundenbuch* as a sort of 'gegerbt Pelzwerk' again with the reference to *Eichhörnchen*! (op.cit. Vol. 22, Register, p. 153).

This is quite impossible. Nowhere have I found evidence that squirrel pelts were tanned 'to make a sack'. How impractical! What sort of tiny tanning instruments have been used in this case? It is, in my opinion, a technical absurdity. In Schiller-Lübben's dictionary (see Vol. 4, p. 84:a) we find the information that 'schevenisse (schevesse, scabenis) abgeschabtes Haar (zum Pelzwerk dienend) Man hat die Haare von den Fellen abgeschabt . . .'. In Latin, it is called *sceuenesses* (in 1252). Nowhere is there the slightest hint of the type of pelt that is meant here. The word appears exclusively in the context of Northern Scandinavian pelt and fur trading, among squirrel, red squirrel pelt, and marten pelt. The consensus is that it is a skin with the hair removed, and, as far as can be told, prepared skin, but no one specifies which skin, except Kunze, who states that it refers to squirrel.

Let us briefly examine the economic situation in Northern Scandinavia at about the end of the 14th century. Reindeer husbandry is in full bloom. Everything points to this fact, for example, the flood of silver to Saami areas, the existence of references to reindeer skins in the Customs lists. At that point in time when we can isolate the Saamis in the Swedish records, that is to say at the beginning of the 16th century, we find rich mountain Saamis with substantial fortunes in silver, a static *sita* organization and highly developed trading. The situation must have been built up and played an active role during the period of lively trading on the North Atlantic coast in the 14th century, trade directed towards England and the Continent. It seems to me to be a reasonable supposition that the Saami family, during their working year, collected prepared reindeer skins, some of the chamois type, some tanned. These would have been easily transported, borne during the summers on the backs of reindeer, and carried over the mountain chain to the mouths of the Northern Norwegian *fiords,* where German and Norwegian ships lay at anchor. Trading took place during the summer. *Schevenisse* refers, in my opinion, to these skins, sometimes tanned, sometimes of the chamois type, which in the Lule Lappish dialect are called *sasné*. There is even a certain phonetic similarity between the Lappish and the Low German words. We are unable to explain the Saami highly developed no-madism and their remarkable economic success unless we are able to trace the means by which they disposed of their goods. But is there anything that could back up my claim that these chamois type and tanned skins went for export? Yes. In the source material from the Hanseatic cities from 1428, there is mention of *vinnische dekene,* that is, Saami 'decks', i.e. 10 reindeer skins (Falk, 1919: 76). It should be noted that the word 'deck' is used in relation to skins, instead of the word 'timmer'. The latter term was used for pelts.

There is yet another term that has not been observed in connection with the Saami fur and skin trade, namely the word *hasenballinge.* It appears in the above-mentioned list from Albert of Bavaria, and else-where. In Schiller-Lübben's dictionary, the word is unexplained, and this is also the case in Kunze's register. Clearly, *hasen* comes from *hosen* (stocking, foot). Reference can be made to Schiller-Lübben, Vol. 2, p. 212. But *Ballinghe* remains an unknown factor. The Lappologist can find the answer close at hand, equating it with the word *belling,* in this case the high quality skin from the reindeer leg, which was sold as a pair, and was used for making shoes. *Hasenbellinghe* ought therefore to be the Low German word for foot, leg, *belling.* As late as in the 19th century, a Saami inventory lists *en omgång bellingar,* a quantity of *bellings.* In the above-mentioned Hanseatic list in which goods were listed regionally, we can find the following goods listed for the Northern Scandinavian area: *schevenesse* (scraped, tanned or possibly chamois type reindeer skin), *hasenballinghe* (reindeer bellings), *sconewerk* (lower quality pelts, for example squirrel pelts), *roet werk* (pelts from the red squirrel, pos-sibly fox), zwart werc (probably from the black cross fox, a valuable item).

Finally, I should like to take up yet another list of goods for analysis. In *Norges gamle love 3* (No 120, p. 221) in the above-mentioned Olaf Haakonssøn's excise list from 1384 concerning the tax on various types of skins: *'af godhom nakka skinnum ij aura . . .'.* In *Glossariet* (part 5) the following explanation is offered: *'nakkaskinn. n.* a sort of skin. Which?' The authors have seemingly been unable to ascertain its origin.

Bendixen (1914–1916, p. 45) takes up this reference and suggests that it may be a misspelling of *rakkeskinn,* referring to *melraake* (white fox) (Aasen, 1918, *Melrakke* = Hvidraev. *Canis Lagopus).* However, before we can assume a misspelling, a check should be made of other mediaeval material to ensure that the word does not appear elsewhere. Turning to German material, we find the following: (from *Wismar In-*

ventarien, 1438–1547, op.cit.) 'Dit sint Joh. de(s) buntmakers nagelaten guder . . . *I woder nachken . . .'.* From another source (Schiller-Lübben, op.cit., Vol. 3, p. 149) we find the passage: 'Das Nackenfell primo exposuit marcas pro duabus particulus, que dicuntur nacken; it XII m. pro III baldichen 1327' (*Mecklenburgisches Urkundenbuch* No 4870 – a.d. 1327).

The term *nackskinn* is thus to be found, but to which animal does it refer? Bendixen suggests, as an alternative to misspelling, 'nakkeskind, vel av ekornens nakke', that is, from the neck of the squirrel (op.cit. p. 45). The solution is probably to be found in the Hanseatic material. In the book *Die ältesten Stadt-Schiff und Landrechte Hamburgs* (publ. J. M. Lappenberg, Hamburg 1845 – 3 R 185 (14)), there is a reference, among others, to 'eyn illekes [polecat] voeder – 39 illeke syn; *vossen voder von nacken und kelen – 24 nackekelen'. Vos* is here the same as the German word *Fuchs, kelen* means throat. In other words, the reference is to neck and throat pelts from fox, referred to as *nackekelen.* (Compare here with the above-mentioned Latin text concerning fine quality neck pelts consisting of two parts, and referred to as *nacken.*) What have these articles been used for? The answer is to be found in the above-mentioned decree in *Norges gamle love* (No 121): 'af godhom nakka skinnum ij aura – firer kapruns foder af hinom baesto skinnom', that is, good quality neck pieces of fox, valued at two *øre,* for use in the lining of hoods, and also a quantity of the best neck pelts. *Kaprun* means hood, that is the hood which was attached to that time's most important outer garment – the cloak. The hood would be lined with fine quality fox fur. The fur on the throat of the fox is fluffy and bushy and would surround the face in an attractive manner. Even in our own time, ladies' fur hats are made of such pelts and constitute the height of fashion.

*

By closely examining mediaeval records against a background of established ethnological material, and by studying the material from a *functional* point of view, placing it in a macroperspective – that is, taking into consideration the prevailing hunting pattern within a particular ecological environment – it is possible to achieve a picture of the society of a bygone age which is as reliable as possible. This in turn gives us a background and a number of points of reference for our further researches into ethnography and into culture relationships in Northern Scandinavia's past. Clearly, ethnologists and archaeologists can profitably exchange material, and philology can provide a valuable support to our research.

Notes

1 From this point of view it is thus misleading to support archaeological analyses concerning *Saami* pelt catches purely on the strength of Ahnlund's work. See, for example, Zachrisson 1976.
2 Ahnlund, 1946: 43, n I. Hultkrantz, 'Svenska kronan och Lappmarkerna under Gustav Vasa'.
3 There is a common view that the catches of beaver pelts were great, as stated by Steckzén in *Birkarlar och lappar* (1964). Compare this view with that presented in the report of the Central Office of National Antiquities (D 9 1975) entitled *Kulturlandskap i älvdalar II* (The Cultural Landscape in the River Valleys II) in which it was stated, with regard to hunting and fishing, that: 'The catches of hunting and fishing were always taxable items during the Middle Ages, and particularly pelts. The most important source of pelts was the squirrel (called *"gråverk"*), the marten and the *beaver* [author's italics]. The Lapps were primarily responsible for the pelt taxes. Domiciled farmers could, however, be in possession of hunting rights far from their home villages.'

The records show, however, that the real picture is quite a different one. From my study of the taxation rolls for pelts relating to the Middle Ages, a period during the 16th century, and the whole of the 17th and 18th centuries, mention of beaver pelts is infrequent, and is even non-existent at times as regards the Swedish Saami areas. In the Finnish Saami areas, the situation is quite different.

Bibliography

Unprinted Sources:

Stockholm: *Nordiska Museet*
Hultkrantz, Å., Svenska kronan och Lappmarkerna under Gustav Vasa.
Umeå: *Dialekt- och ortnamnsarkivet,* Umeå (DAUM)
DAUM: Gr 298 B. Krokträsk, Västerbotten
DAUM: Gr. 525 A. Vilhelmina, Västerbotten
Uppsala: *Universitetsbiblioteket* (UUB)
J. A. Nensén's handskriftssamling
Signum R 649 and R 650

Printed Sources:

Aasen, I.
1873 Norsk Ordbog med dansk forklaring. Christiania.
Ahnlund, N.
1946 Norrländska skinnskatter. Saga och sed 1946: 32–55.
Bendixen, B. E.
1914–16 Vaereomsætningen mellem England og Norge i første halvdel av 14. aarhundrede. (Norsk) Historisk Tidskrift Series 5, vol. 3: 277–313, 444–471.
Bugge, A.
1898 Handelen mellem England og Norge indtil begyndelsen af det 15de aarhundrede. (Norsk) Historisk Tidskrift Series 3, vol. 4: 1–149.
1898–99 Gotlændingernes handel paa England og Norge omkring 1300. (Norsk) Historisk Tidskrift Series 3, vol. 5: 145–180.
1899 Studier over de norske byers selvstyre og handel før Hanseaternas tid. Kristiania.

Diplomatarium Norvegicum
1847–1915 Diplomatarium Norvegicum 1–20 (1). Christiania. (Cit. DN).
Falk, Hj.
1919 Altwestnordische Kleiderkunde. Kristiania.
Fjellström, Ph.
1962 Lapskt silver. Studier över en föremålsgrupp och dess ställning inom lapskt kulturliv. 2 volumes. Uppsala.
Grundström, H.
1946–54 Lulelapsk ordbok. 4 volumes. Skrifter utgivna genom Landsmåls- och folkminnesarkivet i Uppsala, series C. I (1–4). Uppsala.
Hansische Urkundenbücher
1922 Hansische Urkundenbücher, ed. by K. Höhlbaum and K. Kunze. Lübeck.
Högström, P.
1747 Beskrifning öfwer de til Sweriges krona lydande lappmarker. Stockholm.
Lindahl, E. and J. Öhrling
1780 Lexicon Lapponicum. Holmiae (Stockholm).
Mecklenburgisches Urkundenbuch
1907 Mecklenburgisches Urkundenbuch, vol. 22. Schwerin.
Norges gamle love
1846–95 Norges gamle love indtil 1387. 5 volumes. Christiania. (Cit. NGL.)
Riksantikvarieämbetet and Statens historiska museer
1979 Kulturlandskap i älvdalar II. Rapport 1979:2. Stockholm.
Schiller and Lübben
1875–1880 Mittel-niederdeutsches Wörterbuch. 5 Volumes. Bremen.
Steckzén, B.
1964 Birkarlar och lappar. Stockholm.
Zachrisson, I.
1976 Lapps and Scandinavians in Northern Sweden. Early Norrland 10. Stockholm.

III
Hunting Terminology

Through philological and linguistic research the scholar is often able to draw conclusions about earlier hunting conditions. Close investigation of the terminology of a former hunting people may tell us a good deal about hunting implements, techniques and social organization. Pekka Sammal-lahti's paper on Saami hunting terminology is an example of this.

Lappish (Saami) Hunting Terminology in an Historical Perspective

Pekka Sammallahti

In this paper I shall deal with North Lappish (sometimes called Norwegian and Mountain Lappish), which is the major Lappish language. It is spoken by about 80 per cent of all the speakers of the Lappish languages. Furthermore, North Lappish is the central Lappish language influenced by both West European and East European traditions.

Hunting terminology is dependent on several factors: the game available, the methods of catching it, the social structures and processes involved in such catching – including such extrinsic factors as legislation and taxation –, consumption and marketing possibilities, and oral tradition, which serves to preserve obsolete terminology in stories and tales.

As a matter of fact, oral tradition does not seem to be very powerful in preserving old hunting terms. Let me take a few examples. Of the two most important old methods of catching wild reindeer, *bearttuš*[1] or *ákkis* (probably from Finnish *hangas*) and *vuopman,* only the former still has about the same meaning as it used to have when wild reindeer hunting was still actively practised. In this case, however, the technique is, or rather was at the beginning of the century, still used but mainly by thieves catching tame reindeer for sale or consumption. Konrad Nielsen (Nielsen 1932–62) gives the meaning of *bearttuš* (or *bærtoš* in Konrad Nielsen's orthography, henceforth KN) as follows: 'trap between two trees for catching a wild reindeer (or tame reindeer when it is set by thieves, Kr [=Kárašjohka] also a horse), generally with a fence or fences to lead the animals towards the trap.' On the Finnish side, where wild reindeer hunting lasted longer than in the Finnmark plateau, the term *ákkis* still has its original meaning, denoting a rather long fence with openings for traps or falling pits. The second technique called *vuopman* has been completely forgotten and, according to Konrad Nielsen, the word is used in Buolbmat (Norwegian Polmak) only, where it has the meaning 'old Mountain Lapp camping site which can now be used as

103

meadow; the earth there is full of reindeer antlers; indiv.: only known as a place name'. The present meaning of the word probably derives from the place name referred to by Konrad Nielsen (Vorren, oral communication). Originally *vuopman* consisted of two convergent fences leading to a precipice or to an enclosure where the deer were killed. The present meaning of the word *vuopman* is clearly a distant reflection of the killing enclosure with its heaps of reindeer antlers and bones. According to J. Fellman's notes from the early nineteenth century the enclosure was called *soahtegárdi,* which means battle fence.

A third way of catching wild reindeer was hunting, which was practised in the fall and in the winter during crusty snow time. The latter was called something like **muoidi* (Inari Lappish *myeiði* from which Finnish *moita*) and the former *ordu,* because it happened in *orda* or the tree-line in the mountains. *Ordu* is still known in the expression *orddu vázzit* (*vázzit* meaning 'to walk') 'to hunt'. According to Konrad Nielsen, *ordu* (KN *or'do*) means '(illegal) occupation, project (something which dishonest people, reindeer thieves, take to); Karasjok in the obsolete expression *ordo vaʒ'ʒet* go hunting'. In the dialect of Buolbmat the derivative verb *ordet* means 'stay in the mountain with evil intentions (especially of one who is suspected of stealing reindeer'). So the altogether honest and honourable act of hunting wild reindeer has turned into the not so honourable act of stealing tame reindeer. From an historical point of view this is not so surprising.

Let us now turn to the other facets of hunting terminology, namely that of game availability and factors regulating it. There have been two fundamental changes in game availability. The development of extensive reindeer herding for food and exchange goods production caused the wild reindeer stock to turn into privately owned domesticated animals, which could not be hunted legally. This process was completed in about four or five centuries: the last herds of wild reindeer were sighted in the 1920s. In the woodlands wild reindeer hunting was still going on in the nineteenth century, but towards the end of that century it lost its economic significance and even the Forest Saami were actively engaged in reindeer herding with no time left for wild reindeer hunting. The once vital terminology was still alive among the oldtimers of the Inary and Skolt Saamis at the beginning of the twentieth century, but it has subsequently been lost.

One should of course keep in mind that, as pointed out by Bo Wickman (1965), the present domesticated reindeer terminology originates, at least in part, from the days of wild reindeer hunting. Thus we have by and large the same names for reindeer in different ages and sexes throughout the Lappish languages. So what has been forgotten are the names for the activities and equipment which have become superfluous in the process of abandoning hunting for herding. The reason for this transfer, again, is very evident. Wild reindeer hunting was obviously practised in cooperation with other *siidas* or Saami villages, because the hunting grounds lay in the highlands on the *siida* borders. The game was considered jointly owned and open to hunting from both sides of the border. New marketing possibilities created pressures on this rather limited capital, and the need arose to control the consumption of the game more effectively, in this case by making it private property controllable within one family in one *siida*. That the reindeer became privately and not collectively owned was a consequence of the laws concerning the division of catchers: a deer was the property of its catcher or catchers, whereas e.g. a beaver belonged to the whole village or *siida*. Thus a good many old hunting terms live on in a new environment.

So *goddi* or the wild reindeer has turned into *boazu* or the domesticated reindeer and the stock was preserved. But *mádjit* or the beaver did not fare so well; it became extinct at about the same time as the wild reindeer lost its economic significance, i.e. about one century ago. Beaver-catching terminology recorded is extremely sparse (e.g. Skolt *maa'jjikuâ'tt* 'an enclosure under the ice to catch the beaver'), and the last ones to recall some terms were the Skolts, on whose hunting grounds the last beaver was caught. Evidently, one of the factors contributing to the extinction of the beaver was collective ownership combined with the slow disintegration of the *siida* system by an increasing immigration and infiltration of a static peasant population. Today the word *mádjit*, 'beaver', is known mostly from place names in the forest regions. The beaver was a valuable item of taxation and trade and thus heavily hunted.

As the wild reindeer was domesticated for private ownership and the beaver gradually became extinct, other game animals became less and less common and less and less catchable, too. A reaction to this process was the intensification of hunting. Age-old techniques of trapping and snaring were gradually replaced by firearms.

The firearms boom is very clearly reflected in hunting terminology. The oldest large dictionary of Lappish, the one by Knud Leem from 1768, lists many lexical items already obsolete by the time of the next large dictionary in 1887 by J. A. Friis. Friis reflects the situation in the middle of the nineteenth century, but by the first quarter of the twentieth century many of the terms still recorded by Friis have gone out of use, as shown by the largest and most reliable of the Lappish dictionaries, namely the one by Konrad Nielsen. His dictionary materials have been gathered mainly during the first three decades of our century, and now, some fifty years later, the process of specialization with the use of fire-arms has driven several hunting terms out of everyday use, even among the hunters themselves.

A few examples will illustrate the process. Leem gives the noun FUONOS for a wolf pit or a wolf cage. Friis lists the word but states that it is already obsolete (i.e. he has probably taken it from Leem and it had already gone out of use). Nielsen does not have (KN) *fuonos and the word is probably of Finnish origin, c.f. Finnish *huoneus* or *sudenhuone* 'wolf cage'.

Leem's RUSSHJO (probably modern *ruššu) has the meaning 'a thus called machine with which the Saamis catch the little white foxes they call Njāl' (original in Danish). Friis has the same word *ruššo,* but he designates it as dialectical with the meaning '*instrumentum vulpibus albis capiendis'.* Towards the beginning of this century the word was lost, and we don't even know what the trap looked like.

Some of the old terms now have a very restricted geographical distribution although the artifacts they designate either have had or still have a wide distribution. So e.g. Leem's SHJOVTZH 'a thus called machine to catch hares with', also known to Friis (*šovča,* both *šovčča or *šokča in the current orthography), has not been recorded by Nielsen, but it has been noted in Oheejohka (Finnish Utsjoki) just across the border on the Finnish side before World War II in the regular form *šokča* (Itkonen 1948, II: 41). The North Lappish word has cognates in the Lappish languages of the Kola peninsula, so that it must have had a very wide distribution in the old days. The word *šokčat~čokčat~sokčat,* 'be on the watch for someone or something', common even today, is probably of the same origin.

Another example is (KN) *tiei'bmo* recorded in Kárašjohka only, with the meaning 'kind of gin consisting of snares (made of hair) for catching small birds, especially snow-buntings'. The word has been noted down both by Friis and Leem with the same meaning and the technique is well-known even today, but the old word seems to have been lost in the modern language, which has the analytic expression *juovkamuorra* (*juovka* 'tail hair', *muorra* 'stick, piece of wood, tree').

At present, the word *rihta* (KN *ritta* 'trap for catching the larger kinds of beasts of prey') is disappearing as the technique has become unsuccessful. But the process had begun much earlier, as indicated by dictionary records: Leem's dictionary gives the word *Sazhjamasak* 'two pieces of wood one of which is on the right and the other on the left side of the wooden machine which the Lapps call R i t t a'. The term has been lost since and neither Friis nor Nielsen has recorded it.

Two major methods are used in hunting today: snaring and shooting. Snaring (*giella* 'snare' and *giellat* 'to snare') is now limited to willow grouse only, but formerly one was allowed to snare hares as well. Since Nielsen's times, brass wire that easily keeps its shape as a noose has replaced thread as snare material. This has led to a simplification of the snare construction and at least two specific snaring terms have gone out of use: *gávvedat* 'a forked branch for keeping the noose of the grouse snare open', and *boazzi* 'cut, notch cut in the bark of the *gávvedat* where the noose is fastened'. Otherwise the construction has remained the same: the whole fence with a few snares is called *gárdi* (of Scandinavian origin) and to snare with a *gárdi* is called *gárdut*; in the *gárdi* there are openings for snares called (*gárde*)-*uksa* flanked on the one side by a twig called *uksamuorra*; between the snare openings there are lying twigs called *gárderissi* preventing the grouse from passing the construction anywhere but in the snare openings, where they get entangled in the noose. A bundle of snares ready to be set up is called *spáhčč8u*.

Next to snaring in importance comes shooting. The first guns were acquired in the seventeenth century and in three hundred years firearms have replaced bows and arrows, which are now known only as toys but with their names preserved: *dávgi* for the bow and *njuolla* for the arrow. However, the oldest term for the bow, *juoksa,* dating from the Uralic protolanguage, has ben lost in the modern language as well as the name for the crossbow, *juolgedávgi* (*juolgi* 'leg, foot'; cf. Finnish *jalkajousi* 'cross-bow'), recorded by Leem as *juolgge-davggie* but to be found in neither Friis nor Nielsen. Apparently the new shooting equipment has imported new terms as well: a sharpshooter is now called *skuhttar.* The word is of Scandinavian origin, and it has replaced the old word *skuorga* to be found in both Leem and Friis. One who is bad at hitting is called *skuðuheapme* (~*skuruheapme*); the word is derived from something like **skuhtu*, which, in turn, is possibly a deverbal noun from **skuhtit,* which could serve as the base word for *skuhttar* as well. Thus, both *skuhttar* and *skuðuheapme* could be of Scandinavian origin. Firearms have also replaced the spear (*sáiti*) used in bear hunting up to the beginning of the twentieth century. Prior to firearms the spear was used in wild reindeer and wolf hunting as well.

Trapping terminology is still fairly well remembered, although trapping is considered somewhat out-of-date. The different sizes of iron traps with jaws are suitably named according to the type of beast to be caught: the smallest one is called *buoidat-ruovddit* 'ermine trap' (*ruovddit* meaning literally 'irons'), which was used alongside a *gillar* or a small falling trap or a trap with one jaw. Next to it was *njoammelruovddit*, 'hare trap', used besides *giella* 'snare' or *goahta* 'enclosure trap'. The next size was called according to use *čeavraruovddit* 'otter trap' or *riebanruovddit* 'fox trap'. Usually *gumpperuovddit* 'wolf trap' was the biggest of its kind, but some hunters possessed a trap called *guovžžaruovddit* 'bear trap'. In addition to size differences there were different traps according to the way of triggering: the trigger was called *geaŋga* and, if no bait was used, the trap was covered and called *ráðasruovddit*. The bait was pinched on a plate called *skieltu,* in which case the trap was called *skieltoruovddit* 'bait plate trap'. The jaws were called *geavjjat* or *geavllit,* and if they had teeth, the trap was called *bátneruovddit*. Nowadays trapping is – as are many old ways of hunting – becoming more and more the activity of children who may trap small creatures such as mice, jays, and other small birds for fun.

Another method that is almost out of use already is hunting by using poisoned bait. The old word for strychnine *sulimat* (nominative plural of *sulin*) was of Russian origin, suggesting that hunting by using poisoned bait was introduced from the east. Later the word *sulin* has been replaced my *mirko* (~*mirku*), which is of Finnish origin. A poisoned bait is called *seakti,* like any other bait, but false attraction baits are used as well: they are called *sievttas,* derived from the verb *siektat* 'get enticed and accustomed to something, lose one's shyness, fear of someone or something'. One of the reasons for giving up hunting by using poisoned bait was its haphazardness: very often the dogs of the local people fell victims of the bait instead of the wolves, foxes, and gluttons intended.

I have now highlighted some of the present and recent hunting methods and the terminology involved. A few words remain to be said about the social aspects of hunting.

From a social point of view, the acts of hunting and fishing never were so central in the life of the Saami. Their largest social unit, the *siida,* was a territorial unit, most probably an area with the people inhabiting it and sharing common objects of worship and convening for mid-winter for social life in the winter village (Gjessing 1960). The word *siida* is etymologically connected with *sieidi* 'rock or stone which is an object of worship'. Both *siida* and *sieidi* are etymological cognates of the Finnish word *hiisi* (from Pre-Finnic **šite* or perhaps **šijte*), which originally meant a sacrificial grove belonging to one village (cf. Bergsland 1964). So the Saami *siida* was originally more of a worship congregation than a hunting or fishing assembly, and its hunting terminology correlates with society accordingly.

Especially wild reindeer hunting required the collaboration of many families inside the *siida* as well as the coordination of activities between two or more *siida*s in order to organize the big fall hunt or *ordu* in the highlands on the *siida* borders. These modes of collaboration surely created their own terminology, but it has subsequently been lost. Today hunting is mainly the job of a single enterprisers, since in the era of fire-arms the game hunted can quite well be bagged without such big hunting parties as in e.g. elk hunting in more southern areas of Finland and Swe-den. Among the Saamis, though, a couple of hunters usually join each other to face the solitude of the long, cold, and dark winter, the season of the willow grouse hunt, which is then called *searvebivdu* (*searvi* 'com-pany, community, association, society' and *bivdu* 'hunting'). The hunt-ers who have agreed to snare in association or *searvalagaid* share the catch at the end of their hunt. But the word *searvi* (from Finnish *seura* 'club, association, company') is not confined to hunting alone: it can be used of all kinds of associations. So *searvi* is not a hunting term in itself. The members of the *searvi* are rarely more than four in number, but the usual figure is two. In general the members come from the same villages and are thus relatives.

Hunting is a far less important source of livelihood for the Saamis than fishing or later on reindeer husbandry, at least as far as the vast majority of the Saamis – the Forest and Sea Saamis – are concerned. Hunting is not as valuable a food source as fishing, and I am inclined to think that it never was, either. Although it has surely provided the Saamis with great amounts of meat at times, hunting never was such a steady source of food as fishing. Hunting has given the Saamis valuable trade and tax items and provided them with some luxuries such as fur brims and linings for winter caps and occasional palatable morsels in the pot, but fish is everyday food. Among inland Saamis it was only rarely sold or traded, although dried pike seems to have been an important tax item. The central importance of fishing is clearly reflected in the sophistication of its methods and in fishing terminology, which is far richer and far more complicated than hunting terminology, both from a technical and a social point of view. Nevertheless, hunting terminology gives us interesting glimpses into Saami cultural history.

Notes

1 Lappish words will be given in the standard orthography unless they are given in the form in which they appear in the source.

Bibliography

Bergsland, Knut
  1964 Suomen *hiisi.* Virittäja 68: 242–248. Helsinki.
Friis, J. A.
  1887 Lexican Lapponicum. Christianiae.
Gjessing Gutorm
  1960 The Disintegration of the Village Organization of the Sea-Saames (Sea-Lapps). An Hypothesis. Avhandlinger utgitt av Det Norske Videnskaps-Akademi i Oslo. II. Hist.-filos. Klasse. 1960. No. 2. Oslo.
Itkonen, T. I.
  1948 Suomen lappalaiset. I–II. Porvoo.
Leem, Knud
  1768 Lexicon Lapponicum Bipartitum. Nidrosia.
Nielsen, Konrad
  1932–1962 Lappisk ordbok. Lapp Dictionary. I–V. Oslo.
Wickman, Bo
  1965 The Origin of the Lappish Hunting and Fishing Terminology. In Harald Hvarfner (ed.): Hunting and Fishing. Luleå.

IV
Technology and Communication

Aboriginal hunters are travellers. They spend much time in locating the game and in moving with the game. They also visit other people or groups for bartering, feasting, marriage contracts, and similar tasks. Sometimes they make warring expeditions against enemies who live far away. Mostly they are dependent on their own feet for these wanderings. However, many hunters use skis or sledges or boats in order to reach distant places. The arrival of pastoral nomadism with its horse and camel riding facilitated and increased such expeditions, and made occupations of new areas possible.

The two papers in this section underline the role of communications in hunting societies. Helge Larsen describes and analyses the origins of some means of transportation in northern North America, the snowshoe, the sled and the canoe. Johannes Falkenberg's contribution is a study of the ways in which the wanderings of Australian aborigines are related to the acquisition of cultural objects owned or produced by other tribal groups and local clans. Whereas the Eskimo and Indian cases adduced by Larsen clearly fall in line with the hunting horisons hitherto represented in this volume – the hunting cultures of the northern hemisphere –, the Australian materials present an interesting, deviant form of hunting culture. The Falkenberg paper stands as a healthy corrective to the view that a knowledge of Circumboreal hunting customs is sufficient for our understanding of the way of life of ancient hunters. In fact, the northern tradition represents one hunting culture out of several.

Eskimo and Indian Means of Transport, their Relationships and Distribution

Helge Larsen

My contribution to the Symposium is based on some unusual archaeological finds I made in Alaska 30 years ago. The finds were made at Deering, a now almost abandoned Eskimo village in the southern part of Kotzebue Sound. Merely by chance I discovered here the well-preserved remains of a house, which appeared to belong to the Ipiutak culture and which on account of its unusually large size has been interpreted as a men's house, a *qalegi*. I shall refrain from describing the construction of the house and the actual excavation and only emphasize the extremely good preservation of organic materials. Owing to the fact that prior to the excavation the ground had been permanently frozen for more than 1000 years, all kinds of organic materials and in particular a huge amount of wood were preserved. At Point Hope, where the first and so far largest find of Ipiutak culture was made, the preservation of antler, walrus ivory, and bone were generally good, but wooden objects were relatively rare, and it is just wooden objects we are dealing with here.

Three cultural elements represented in the find, namely the snowshoe, the sled, and the boat, have played an important role in the life of arctic hunters and, as it appears from the following, are of special interest on account of their distribution. As far as the snowshoe is concerned, all scholars agree that this cultural element does not originally belong in the Eskimo culture and where snowshoes do occur among Eskimos they are, according to Birket-Smith, 'anything but more or less successful imitations of the snowshoes of the neighbouring Indians' (Birket-Smith 1929 II: 36). It is also the general assumption that the Eskimos adopted the snowshoe relatively late; thus Murdoch says that snowshoes were not common at Point Barrow until the middle of the nineteenth century (Birket-Smith 1929 II: 36). However, archaeological investigations have later proven that Eskimos in Alaska have used snowshoes much earlier; thus there is evidence of the use of snowshoes on the Kobuk in the fif-

A selection of artifacts from the Ipiutak site at Deering. The three specimens at the bottom are: a snowshoe cross-piece, the toy canoe, and the runner of a toy sled (from Geografisk Tidsskrift).

teenth to eighteenth centuries (Giddings 1952), from the thirteenth century at Nukleet in Norton Sound (Giddings 1964), and at Point Hope from the time of the Western Thule Culture (Larsen and Rainey 1948, Pl. 88.10).

The find from Deering shows not only that Eskimos had snowshoes at least as far back as 5–600 A.D., but also that these snowshoes are anything but primitive imitations of those of their Indian neighbours, the Athapaskans. Actually, the comparison must be made with Athapaskan snowshoes from historic times, because we do not know of any prehistoric ones. In other words, because Eskimo snowshoe-parts are older than any Athapaskan snowshoes, we cannot say whether they are good or bad imitations, or whether they are imitations at all. On the other hand, one may say that the snowshoes of the Ipiutak culture are in many ways similar to a certain type of snowshoe which Davidson in his monograph on snowshoes designates as an Athapaskan type. According to

Davidson's classification, the Ipiutak snowshoe is an Athapaskan type characterized by a two-piece frame with pointed toe and pointed heel, with rectangular netting between two crossbars, and the netting fastened to the frame through horizontal holes (Davidson 1937, Fig. 32). This last feature is important, because it limits the distribution of this type to an area between the Mackenzie district in the east and the northeast corner of Siberia in the west (Davidson 1937, Fig. 13). Davidson's classification and maps of distribution are of course based on ethnographical materials, and we do not know what the distribution was like 13–1400 years ago. Neither do we know for sure who were the originators, the Athapaskans or the Eskimos, although I must admit that I consider the Indians as the most likely.

The sled was also a surprise. At Point Hope we had found a few flat pieces of wood, which, because their shape reminded us of bone sled shoes of the Central Eskimos, we cautiously suggested were parts of the Ipiutak people's sleds. The Deering find gave us ample proof that our interpretation that the pieces from Point Hope were parts of sleds was correct; they were not, however, sled shoes to fasten under the runners but the runners themselves. Because it is the first time such runners occur in an archaeological find, there are certain uncertainties regarding the reconstruction of this hitherto unknown sled form. A reconstruction has been attempted based on fragments of runners, the longest of which is 89 cm, and on four more or less complete runners of toy sleds, which we must assume represent sleds for grown-ups on a reduced scale. The runners are shaped as skis, 5–7 cm wide and 2–2.5 cm thick, but their characteristic feature is a 11–12 cm high stanchion placed about 30 cm from the rear end and carved out of the same piece of spruce as the rest of the runner. A cross-piece has been placed on top of the stanchion as a connection between the two runners; a wooden arch further ahead has formed another connection. In front the runners were turned up and probably connected. We do not have any indication of the platform that must have rested on the cross-piece and the arch, but enough to tell us that the Ipiutak sled was a built-up sled. It was apparently a small sled, probably less than 2 m long, and we do not know whether or not it was pulled by dogs. We do know, however, that the Ipiutak people had dogs.

As was the case with the snowshoe, the finding of the sled parts calls for a revision of former views regarding the types of Eskimo sleds. Thus Birket-Smith says that 'the built-up sledge is a recent loan from the other side of the Bering Strait' (Birket-Smith 1929 II: 72). It is, of course, a question of what he concidered 'recent', and considering that built-up sleds in the Old World probably go back to the Stone Age, even A.D. 600 is late, and we do not even know whether the Ipiutak sled represents the earliest occurrence in the New World of this type of sled. In his work, corresponding to Davidson's on the snowshoes, Gösta Berg has given a thorough description of sled types and their distribution (Berg 1935: Pl. 9, 2). Among his types are also forms with runners similar to those from Deering, with a Stanchion carved out of the same piece of wood, but considering that the sleds in question are timber-sleds from Sweden used in historic times, there is hardly any connection with the Ipiutak sled. Another equally doubtful connection is with a sled model from Ungava Bay that has the same kind of runners, but which is almost as far east of Alaska as Sweden is to the west (Mason 1896: 572 and fig. 260).

It is likely, however, that there is a connection between sled forms that have the platform resting either on arches alone or with additional posts. Sleds with these characteristics are only known from a limited area, namely the north-easternmost part of Asia and Alaska, that is largely the same area in which the Ipiutak form of snowshoes occurred. The Asiatic forms have flat runners similar to those from Deering; the arches are either of wood or antler. Arches of antler are known from the Birnirk culture from about A.D. 800, and because this culture is known from as far west as Kolyma, they were probably also used there at that time or earlier. In Alaska the built-up sled is used by most Eskimos from the Bering Strait to the Mackenzie though in a highly developed form, with rails to support the load even if simpler forms are known. It is, however, particularly interesting that some of the Athapaskan neighbours of the Eskimos, such as the Kutchin, the Han, Tanana, and Ingalik have or are known to have had sleds of the same general type, undoubtedly taken over from the Eskimos.

Finally, we have the third cultural element, the boat, and I say expressly boat and not kayak or canoe because it is something in between. My only definite proof that the Deering people knew of and probably used a vessel, is the model of a boat, 22 cm long, a little over 2 cm wide and high, carved out of cottonwood. It is flat-bottomed, pointed at both ends, and, what is particularly interesting, with the central part hollowed-out to a depth of 1 cm, leaving 5 cm at the bow and 3 cm at the stern flat as if they were decked. In the middle of the boat, which is painted red, a coarse carving does duty as a man.

There is no doubt that we are dealing with the model of a so-called kayak-form canoe, a type of canoe described by Adney and Chapelle in

The Bark Canoes and Skin Boats of North America, but also mentioned by other authors. The kayak-form canoes are 4–6 m long and 60–70 cm wide, flat-bottomed boats with pointed ends and partly decked at the bow and usually also at the stern. Birch-bark was the most common material for this type of canoe. They were light and primarily used for hunting in rivers and lakes. The hunter, using a single or a double paddle, was usually kneeling in the centre of the boat and often had his weapons placed below the bow deck.

Kayak-form canoes were used by practically all the northern Athapaskans, from Ingalik in the West to the Chipewyan in the East, but also by some of their Eskimo neighbours, as for instance the Kobuk Eskimos, who live not far from Deering. There can be no doubt that the Ipiutak people used a vessel that corresponded in shape to the kayak-form canoe; the question is whether it was covered with bark. Numerous pieces of birch-bark were found in and around the Deering house, but they were all too small to be used as cover for a boat. If the Deering people built bark canoes, they would have had to travel at least 240 km as the crow flies to find birch trees large enough to produce bark of sufficient size, and it would have been quite impossible for the Eskimos of the Birnirk culture at Barrow, who apparently have used the same kind of boats (Birket-Smith 1929 II: 172). It is more likely that the kayak-form canoes used by the Ipiutak and Birnirk people were covered by skin. In support of this assumption I may mention that two rather large pieces of seal skin with watertight seams, which could very well have been boat covers, were found at Deering. Kayak-form canoes covered with skin are also known from the Athapaskans; thus Birket-Smith writes about the Chipewyan Indians that, when they are on the Barren Grounds in the summer, they cover their canoes with caribou skin when they cannot get birch-bark (Ford 1959: fig. 78 d).

The facts stated above raise two questions. Because of the conformity regarding materials, construction, and shape between the kayak-form canoes of the Athapaskans and the Kobuk Eskimos, there can be no doubt about their common origin; the question is where? It must have originated in an area where birch-bark is easily accessible and in sufficient quantities, that is in a boreal forested area like that inhabited by the Athapaskans while most of the Eskimos live outside the forest. Meanwhile, before we draw the conclusion that this type of boat originated in Alaska, we must not forget that birch-bark canoes closely resembling the kayak-form canoe also occur in eastern Siberia, for instance among the Goldi, the Evenk, and at the mouth of the Amur. The partly covered

Ipiutak boat also raises the question formulated by Gudmund Hatt in 1916, namely whether the birch-bark canoe could be the prototype of the kayak? Finally, a third question could be raised on the basis of these comments on the means of transport of the Ipiutak people: is it a coincidence that all three elements, the snowshoe, the sled, and the canoe, occur in similar forms in a limited area on both sides of the Bering Strait or is there a connection? In my opinion the latter is the most likely.

Bibliography

Adney, Edwin Tappan and Howard I. Chapelle
    1964 The Bark Canoes and Skin Boats of North America. – Smithsonian Institution, U.S. National Museum, Bull. 230, Washington D.C.
Berg, Gösta
    1935 Sledges and Wheeled Vehicles. – Nordiska Museets Handlingar: 4, Stockholm and Copenhagen.
Birket-Smith, Kaj
    1929 The Caribou Eskimos I – II. – Report of the Fifth Thule Expedition, Vol. V, Copenhagen.
Davidson, D. S.
    1937 Snowshoes. – Memoirs of the American Philosophical Society, Vol. VI, Philadelphia.
Ford, James A.
    1959 Eskimo Prehistory in the Vicinity of Point Barrow, Alaska. – Anthropological Papers of the American Museum of Natural History, Vol. 47, Pt. 1, New York.
Giddings, J. L. jr.
    1952 The Arctic Woodland Culture of the Kobuk River. – Museum Monographs, The University Museum, Philadelphia.
    1964 The Archaeology of Cape Denbigh. – Brown University Press, Providence R. I.
Hatt, Gudmund
    1916 Moccasins and their Relation to Arctic Footwear. – Memoirs of the American Anthropological Association, Lancaster.
Larsen, Helge
    1951 De dansk-amerikanske Alaska-ekspeditioner 1949–50. – Geografisk Tidsskrift, Vol. 51, Copenhagen.
Larsen, Helge and Froelich Rainey
    1948 Ipiutak and the Arctic Whaling Culture. – Anthropological Papers of the American Museum of Natural History, Vol. 42, New York.
Mason, Otis T.
    1896 Primitive Travel and Transportation. – Report of the U.S. National Museum for 1894, Washington D.C.

Tribe, Material Culture, and Communication among the Murinbata of Northern Australia

Johannes Falkenberg

I

The concept of the tribe has various different meanings in anthropological literature, but if we limit our definition to apply to Australia only, we may define the tribe as a group of people possessing the same language and the same culture. The tribe also has a local aspect, as its language and culture characterize the population of a connected area. Finally, the tribe and its members bear a distinct (tribal) name. The Murinbata tribe (see sketch-map Fig. 1), with which we are here concerned, is an example of such a group. The members of this tribe have no common ancestor, and they are genealogically, politically, and economically no more intimately linked to each other than to members of other tribes. They are not united by any specific tribal interests which might give them common privileges or common obligations. They have no central leadership, and the tribe never gathers in order to carry out any kind of common tribal task. But even so, they form an entity of language and of culture, and the purpose of the present account is to attempt to explain the factors responsible for the existence and maintenance of this entity.

It seems reasonable to assume that the linguistic and cultural unity of the tribe must be the result of extensive communication between those people who, together, form this group. But what kind of communication between the Aborigines has resulted in the formation of the Murinbata tribe, clearly distinguished from other tribes?

I shall make the assertion that the particular communication between the Aborigines which eventually led to the establishment of the Murinbata tribe has its point of departure in the geographical distribution of the local clan totems, and below I shall attempt to verify this hypothesis.

119

But first I would point out that local clan totems are closely connected with particular totem-sites and that hundreds of such totem-sites are scattered over the Port Keats district. Furthermore, a given series of neighbouring local totem-sites constitutes a local clan area associated with a particular local clan, and each tribal territory is divided into a number of such local clan areas. The country around and between the totem-sites of a given local clan area may be referred to as a horde territory and is, normally, occupied by a particular horde. It should be emphasized that whereas the clan area is a sacred area, the horde territory may be characterized as a profane tract of land.

The horde, which, normally, consists of the men whose clan area lies within their horde territory, and their wives and children, is the land-occupying and land-utilizing group. While the horde is tied economically to its horde territory, the members of a local clan are bound by common spiritual ties to their local clan area. Furthermore, while the members of a horde, normally, live together in their horde territory and have everyday relations with each other, the members of a local clan live apart, since the clan's women are married into alien hordes.

It should be noted that even though all the members of a given local clan are intimately tied to their own local clan area by a series of local clan totems, it is the adult, initiated men of the clan who are the custodians of the sacred totems. These totems are, however, also of great importance to members of other local clans, and there is therefore extensive communication between members of different local clans.

As an illustration of the role played by the local clan totems with regard to communication between people in the Port Keats district, I shall first consider a local clan by the name of Nanabägor, whose clan area lies close to the actual Murinbata territory (see sketch-map Fig. 1). The Nanabägor clan has more than 40 local totems, and one of these is that of the common headache. The home of the headache is a certain totem-site in Nanabägor, known as Rambu, where there are a multitude of headache spirits, who from time to time break away from Rambu and settle in the heads of the people of Nanabägor and of others. We should add here that the common headache is one of the most frequent disorders among the Aborigines, who often suffer from it badly.

When a headache spirit has entered the head of a person, it will stay there and play havoc for a while, before returning to Rambu. But at times such a headache can become so troublesome that the sufferer requires immediate help, and no one is able to render the patient better help than the initiated men from Nanabägor. Therefore, one must get in touch with these men; either a messenger is sent off to fetch one of them, or the patient himself, usually accompanied by a couple of others, goes to Nanabägor. Here a skilled person will pull some hair out of the patient's head and from his armpits. These hairs are singed over a slow fire, and rubbed on the patient's chest, back, and head. What is left of the hair after this is stuffed into the patient's nostrils, and he will start to get better the very next day. After another day or two, he will be entirely restored.

As we are at present concerned only with the communication aspect of local totemism, we must add that even though the interaction described above is caused by the headache, the social contact between the patient and the men of Nanabägor will lead to consequences far beyond the actual treatment of the disorder. For as the cure takes its course, the patient and the people of Nanabägor will communicate also about many matters which have nothing to do with the headache, and finally their interest will no longer be focused on this. The patient will talk about many subjects concerning his own local group, and in return he will receive information about what is taking place in Nanabägor. And when he comes home, his own group will for quite some time be entertained with news from Nanabägor. In this way a headache can trigger off extensive communication; as this ailment strikes most of the Aborigines at some time or other, practically all those living in the Port Keats district will at various times seek direct contact with the people of Nanabägor.

Whereas headache is associated with only one specific locality of the Port Keats district, there are other local totems linked to two, three or more localities in the district. This is of great practical importance, because it makes for shorter lines of communication in certain cases. To give an example: blood is a local totem belonging to Madjelindi, Idiji-Naninj and Jeder (see sketch-map Fig. 1). If, for instance, a man has been wounded by a spear and has lost much blood, it is of great importance that contact should not only be established with someone who has blood as a local totem, and who therefore holds command over all blood and is thus able to stop any bleeding, but that it should be established as quickly as possible. Therefore it is of paramount importance that speedy help from Madjelindi, Idiji-Naninj or Jeder is available wherever within the Port Keats district someone has lost blood.

Blood and headache are merely two random instances of the great variety of local totems to be found within the Port Keats district. We have cited them here merely in order to illustrate the significance of local totems from the point of view of communication. But in order to be able to understand the tremendous importance of these totems for inter-action between the Aborigines, one must view all the local totems as one coherent entity. It should be noted that a human being is never considered as a local totem, but otherwise practically everything which, according to the beliefs of the Murinbata, is an active, living phenome-non, is a local totem, and there are hundreds of such totems throughout the Port Keats district. However, all these totems, as well as many others, also exist outside this district: according to the Murinbata, the whole world is divided into local totem groups, and each totem is re-lated to an infinite number of different places and groups. Headache, for instance, is not only associated with one specific place in the Port Keats district. As the Murinbata see it, this totem, like all other local totems, is linked to an infinite number of different localities, spread over the whole world at certain intervals. In this way all people are able to come into contact with persons associated with the very sources of life, i.e. with all those forces which are of vital importance if life is to run its normal course.

If, therefore, a particular continuous district itself possesses the most important local totems, people from that district will not need to travel outside it in order to establish local totem contacts with other people. As a result, direct communication between the people living here will be extremely intimate, and it is obvious that such close contact between people of so restricted a district must, in the course of time, lead to consequences affecting those who are associated with one another in this way.

It should be added, however, that a district of reasonable size can hardly be entirely self-supporting as concerns local totems. Therefore there will normally be a need for some totem contacts outside the dis-trict too. These more distant contacts, which may, because of the dis-tances involved, be indirect, employing a varying number of middlemen, are immaterial in the present context. The point is that the very pre-requisite for the cultural unity within a district is not the totem contacts per se, but the special distribution of loal totems within the district.

The question is: is there within the limited tribal territory of the Murinbata so great a variety and so great a number of local totems that one would be justified in describing the Murinbata as being largely self-supporting in the matter of local totems? Or, is there within the Murinbata territory a number of local totems of such importance that they lead to comprehensive contact between the Aborigines living there?

If this is so, we may conclude that the linguistic and cultural unity of the Murinbata is largely a result of the geographical distribution of the local clan totems within the Port Keats district.

On the sketch-map shown below, the Fitzmaurice River represents the southern limit of the Murinbata tribal territory; the stippled line denotes the northern and eastern limits, while the coast forms the western limit. The distribution of the local clan areas within the Murinbata territory is roughly indicated on the map:

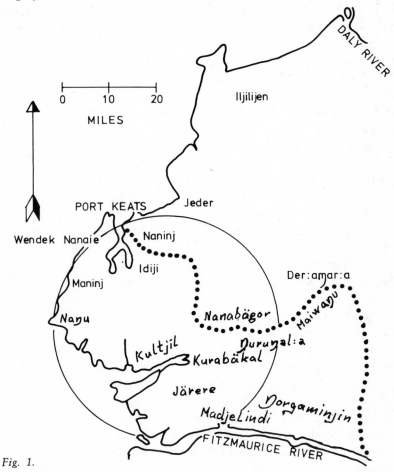

Fig. 1.

It should be noted that none of the easternmost clan areas – Maiwaŋu, Ŋuruŋal:a and Ŋorgaminjin – are ancient Murinbata areas. Ŋorgaminjin, for instance, belonged formerly to a tribe whom the Murinbata call Murinwumeri, while Ŋuruŋal:a and Maiwaŋu belonged to the Mariŋar tribe.

What actually happened to the local clans associated with these three areas is not quite clear. In 1950, the Murinbata told me that most of the members of these local clans had either died or had moved to Darwin, to cattle stations or elsewhere before 1935, the year the mission was established, and that Murinbata-speaking people had taken over their territories.

But how had this take-over of territory come about? In 1950 I was able to ascertain that there had, in the course of time, been contracted aa great number of marriages between the people of Maiwaŋu, Ŋuruŋal:a and Ŋorgaminjin, on the one hand, and members of quite a few Murinbata clans on the other. Thus, the fact that the Murinbata culture and language gained a foothold among these three local groups may largely be a result of these alliances. However, after some years the Murinbata also left these areas, moving to cattle stations, peanut farms etc., and by 1950 the three areas were completely deserted.

The above may indicate that intermarriage, combined with a decimation of the population of certain territories, may make it possible for an alien tribe to expand and to influence the language and culture of the population of a territory that had not previously belonged to this alien tribe. However, in the present context the problem is not how a tribe can expand and increase its population and territory at the expence of other tribes; our interest is focussed on the more general problem of how a tribe is established as a separate linguistic and cultural entity. For this reason we shall disregard the three dispersed clans Maiwaŋu, Ŋuruŋal:a and Ŋorgaminjin, which once belonged to the Mariŋar or the Murinwumeri tribe; instead we shall concentrate on the local clans which, within living memory, formed part of the Murinbata tribe.

On the sketch-map above we have drawn a circle with a radius of 25 miles around Kultjil; all the old, established clan areas of the Murinbata lie within this circle: Idiji, Wendek Nanaie, Maninj, Naŋu, Kultjil, Kurabäkal, Järere and Madjelindi. But there are also two other local clan areas within this circle: Naninj, which belongs to the Magatige tribe, and Nanabägor, which belongs to the Mariŋar.

The distances between the local clan areas within this circle are so small that a Murinbata can come into contact with any camp inside the circle in the course of one or two days. The same applies to the members of the Naninj and Nanabägor local clans. But as Naninj and Nanabägor both lie on the outskirts of the area, and as the members of these two local clans live at a short distance also from other clan areas beyond the

124

circle, the means of communication open to them are far more numerous than is the case for the members of most of the Murinbata clans.

A single example should suffice to illustrate this: the set of local totems of the Murinbata clan Järere and of the Mariŋar clan Der:aŋar:a both include the black duck and a special kind of water-lily, while the Murinbata clans Kultjil and Naŋu as well as the Mariŋar clan Der:aŋar:a all include the yellow duck, the white duck, and a different kind of water-lily among their local totems. Thus, if members of the Nanabägor local clan for some important reason or other wish to communicate with people who have the black duck, the white duck, the yellow duck, or one of the above water-lilies among their local totems, it is easier for them to contact people from Der:aŋar:a rather than people from Järere or from Kultjil-Naŋu. Even though the members of the Nanabägor and Naninj clans certainly are in close contact with the Murinbata, they are in still more intimate contact with members of their own tribe, and for this reason they are not included in the present account.

II

There are a great number of totem sites spread throughout the various local clan areas belonging to the Murinbata tribe. Together they form the home of more than 200 local totems, comprising series of various animals, fish, birds, insects, trees, shrubs, plants, fruit, roots, celestial bodies, elemental forces such as lightning, thunder, etc., fire, water, tools, weapons, diseases, etc.

The local totems are of great importance to the Aborigines in various cultural and social contexts, but naturally we cannot examine each and every one of these totems here, nor is this necessary for our purposes. We can illustrate the problem under consideration by means of a random sample, and for practical reasons we shall restrict our discussion to those totems which are elements of the material culture of the Murinbata tribe. It is of no consequence for our purposes, however, that the Aborigines themselves do not regard their material culture (in the sense of weapons, tools, adornment, and other objects) as a separate category of phenomena, for they classify the phenomena surrounding them as living and dead, not as material and spiritual. Thus, according to the Aborigines' traditional point of view a tool is material as well as spiritual.

A survey of these totemic objects will enable us to establish the extent to which the Murinbata can meet their own requirements as regards essential weapons, tools and other objects by way of contact with people within their own tribal district. This is an important point, for the Aborigines are always in need of these vitally important articles, for which there is a constant and enormous demand.

But even though material objects form the focal point of discussion, the present analysis is concerned with only one single aspect of the Murinbata artifacts, i.e. that of communication. Thus, we shall examine not the objects as such, their form and function, but the circumstances surrounding them. These then are the questions of primary concern in the present context: Can we find evidence to show that the objects most important to the Murinbata are local clan totems within their own tribal territory? Is the system behind the production and distribution of these objects such as to explain the fact that intercommunication between the Murinbata is more extensive, more profound, than communication between the Murinbata and other tribes?

As we shall be dealing only with totemic artifacts, and not with any of the other local totems, we must add a few words about the Aborigines' conception of objects, and of material values generally. What do they understand by an object, a tool, a weapon? In *Economic Structure and the Ceremonial Exchange Cycle in Arnhem Land* (1949), Donald F. Thomson points out that the Aborigines of Arnhem Land differentiate clearly between those objects which they call *märdai'inboi,* and those known to them as *wäkkinŋu.* This distinction is most significant. According to Thomson, objects classified as *märdai'inboi* include 'all things entitled to be termed *yarkomirri,* which means that they are sacred by reason of dedication to, or association with a totemic ancestor or a clan totem'. These objects include certain armlets and weapons, tools, articles of adornment, etc., ornamented with totemic clan patterns. But the essential property of these objects is the fact that they possess *marr,* a very powerful spiritual force.

Those objects which are known as *wäkkinŋu* are of an entirely different order. Again according to Thomson, the word *wäkkinŋu* means 'rubbish, uncouth, outlandish', but that must not be taken to mean that such objects are without any value. Thus, a woman's digging stick, her baskets, and all her other possessions are *wäkkinŋu,* as are also a man's ordinary weapons, his canoe, his fishing net – in fact, all his personal, everyday equipment. Finally, woollen blankets, mosquito nets, and other goods which the Aborigines obtain from the white man are also known as *wäkkinŋu.* The fact that an object is *wäkkinŋu* indicates primarily that it has no connection with mythology. No deference, veneration or

126

respect is connected with such an item, although it can certainly be very much in demand and of great practical importance.

Even so, we must add that an object of the type *wäkkinηu* is never of quite the same great practical value as a corresponding object of the type *märdai'inboi*. Although the importance of objects of the type *märdai'inboi* is mainly connected with their role in the ceremonial life of the Aborigines, many of them are also of great practical value in everyday life. Thus, a spear that is described as *märdai'inboi* will, for instance, endow the hunter with sharp sight and good fortune in the hunt, while a *wäkkinηu* spear does not possess these much-coveted properties.

The material culture of the Murinbata, too, can be divided into two categories, which we may perhaps term sacred and profane. However, the distinction between sacred and profane objects is not entirely the same among the Murinbata as among the people of Arnhem Land. All objects which are local totems, or *ηakumal* as the Murinbata themselves call them, occupy about the same position as that of the objects known to the people of Arnhem Land as *märdai'inboi*. According to Thomson, the term *märdai'in* is, in fact, 'the ordinary or "outside" name for a clan totem'. But the Murinbata category of *ηakumal* includes a far greater number of objects than those classified as *märdai'inboi* by the people of Arnhem Land. As we have seen, a woman's digging stick and basket, and the daily weapons and the fishing net of a man, are known as *wäkkinηu* among the people of Arnhem Land, and thus these objects are profane in their view; all such things are, however, classified as *ηakumal* by the Murinbata, and are thus sacred.

Whereas the Murinbata and the people of Arnhem Land classify a number of their own traditional objects in different ways, they classify all articles which they obtain from the white man, or which are a result of the white man's influence, in the same way. All such items, which are not rooted in the Aborigines' own culture, and which the people of Arnhem Land call *wäkkinηu* ('rubbish'), are profane also among the Murinbata. Their very form distinguishes them clearly from the Murinbata's own traditional products, and regardless of whether one is thinking of textiles, blankets, mosquito nets, steel axes or yet other objects, they are all utility articles whose functions are purely practical.

While a number of the white man's goods have been taken into use by the Murinbata, many of their own, traditional objects have disappeared completely or have been replaced by new, foreign articles. To take an example: at the beginning of the present century, during the childhood of some of my informants, stone axes and knives were in common use among the Murinbata, but they have long since been replaced by steel axes and knives.

On the other hand, the Murinbata today produce certain items which they did not make before. Thus, they make special articles intended to be bartered in exchange for tobacco at the Mission Station. The head of the Port Keats Mission Station in fact initiated this production. He was most enthusiastic about activating the Aborigines in as many ways as possible. Not only did he encourage them to be faithful to their own traditions, but he also induced them to produce entirely new things, and to decorate them with carved, painted, or burnt-in, designs. As he gave tobacco to those who did good work, many of the Aborigines started making special shields, clubs, gathering troughs, etc., decorated with naturalistic or geometric patterns. But even though these products are largely based on the Aborigines' own traditional style, they nevertheless differ from the old Murinbata objects. During my stay at Port Keats in 1950 I acquired more than a hundred such 'mission objects'; I first took them to be genuine Murinbata artifacts, but my informants later described them as 'rubbish'.

Moreover, at the Mission Station the Aborigines are taught to make various things, such as rugs etc., which are entirely foreign to their own, traditional culture. These products, as well as those described above, which are made primarily for the purpose of being exchanged for tobacco, are all due to impulses from the Mission Station. However, even before 1935, when the Mission Station was established, barter with their neighbours had acquainted the Aborigines with certain industrially produced articles, such as woollen blankets, mosquito nets, and iron axes and knives. All these objects, which have been incorporated into the culture of the Aborigines in different ways and at different times, and whose presence is a result of contact with the white man, share one common aspect: they are not rooted in the old Murinbata culture. They have all either come from the white man, or they were made as a result of the white man's influence. And just as a Murinbata will not normally address a white man with a so-called kinship term, he will not refer to an object made by the white man, or made as a result of his influence, by a kinship term.

This is an important aspect of the cultural process of change undergone by the Murinbata. It should be noted that in their traditional social universe, trees and flowers, animals, birds, fish, celestial bodies, tools, weapons and adornments were integrated into the Murinbata kinship system, just as human beings were. Thus, a tool or a weapon was re-

128

ferred to by a kinship term, just like a human being. But objects manufactured by the white man, or produced as a result of contact with the
white man, have not been so fully integrated into the culture of the
Murinbata that they are associated with Aboriginal mythology and ceremonial life, in which human beings, animals, plants, and objects are
bound to each other with social kinship ties.

Before the arrival of the white man, all the Murinbata artifacts were
sacred. The women's digging sticks, their collecting bags, etc. were
sacred in the same sense as all other objects, or more precisely, they were
local clan totems. As late as the beginning of the twentieth century,
when many of my informants were children, practically the entire material culture of the Murinbata was still sacred. But in the course of the
last few decades, the import of new goods and articles deriving from the
white man has led to an entirely new conception of what an object actually represents, and of the essential functions associated with various
objects. As the import of new goods increased, the Aborigines' interest
became more and more concerned with the outer, material qualities of an
object. Naturally, all could see that blankets or mosquito nets, although
not sacred, were items of great practical value, and this more 'material-
istic' conception gradually led to a demythologization of the Aborigines'
own products. This process of secularization is what really matters, not
the fact that steel axes superseded stone axes, that stone spear-heads
were replaced by spear-heads of iron, etc.

The process of disintegration here indicated was already well under
way in 1950. True, to some extent the Aborigines of Port Keats still
used weapons, tools, and personal adornments of the traditional type,
together with a number of new objects; these traditional articles were
still formally classified as ŋakumal or local totems, and many of them
were still important elements in the people's sacred ceremonies. But a
number of traditional artifacts were no longer associated with Aboriginal
mythology and ceremonial life. Their social significance had been reduced
drastically, because they had to a considerable extent been transformed
into purely utility articles and were now often made by people who
would, in the past, have been entitled to use them, but not to produce
them. Even though many of these objects still retained the traditional
form, they had undergone an essential transformation in the mind of the
Aborigines. Once they had been regarded as living creatures who were
referred to by kinship terms, but now they were reduced to dead things
solely intended for practical use and without social kinship relations with
the world around.

III

In 1950 the material culture of the Murinbata was undergoing a process of change which involved a clash between things old and new, between tradition and alien impulses. Above we have in general terms discussed certain aspects of the material culture of the Murinbata at this date. In what follows we shall disregard the non-totemic objects and solely concentrate on the traditional artifacts in their capacity of local clan totems, for only the totemic objects associated with Murinbata local totem sites, and their production and distribution, are of consequence to the establishment and maintenance of the Murinbata tribe. It should be added that, for the sake of convenience, the present tense is used below, even though a great deal of the account refers to the recent past.

In general it may be said that the traditional material culture of the Australian Aborigines is remarkably simple, but even so it plays a very great role in the lives of the Aborigines. Particularly objects associated with collecting, hunting, fishing, fighting and ceremonies are of paramount importance if life is to take its normal course.

There is a great demand for such items in all Murinbata camps. Surprisingly enough even though their material culture comprises few things, no Murinbata camp is self-supporting in the matter of essential artifacts. Some local clans in fact do not produce any objects at all. When I stayed at Port Keats in 1950 I asked some adult men to make various traditional articles, things they themselves possessed and used every day, but the result was so dismal as to make it perfectly clear that these men had never before made such things. They admitted this, adding that these objects belonged to other areas.

And this is an important point. The work is technically so easy that a Murinbata should most certainly be able to make any of the few, simple, objects which he requires. But it should be noted that the production of an object requires more than simply the technical ability to make it. As mentioned above, the Murinbata conceive all (sacred) objects as living beings. Such things are not made, they are born, live, die and are reborn, in a never-ending cycle, in the same way as headaches, blood, human beings, animals, plants, etc. The visible part of such an object is, to the Murinbata, simply an outer shell around an inner, invisible core which the Murinbata call *njäpan,* and which might perhaps be said to be the 'spirit' of this object. It is because of these different *njäpan* that things like spears, clubs, digging sticks, collecting bags, etc. are of particular value, since a *njäpan* is an active spiritual force which endows the

130

object with life and with efficaciousness. These ideas are highly reminiscent of the Arnhem Land concept of *marr,* which we discussed above. According to the Murinbata, only the outer shell of an object perishes, while its inner core or 'spirit' possesses eternal life. Therefore, what we conceive of as an object is, to the Murinbata, not the entire article, not even its most vital part, but merely the outer, material manifestation of the object. This dualistic view of an object must be clearly understood, because it is the very key to an understanding of the material culture of the Aborigines of the Port Keats district.

Just like blood, headaches, and many other phenomena, all (sacred) objects are intimately connected with certain totem sites, and one might say that their association with these sites is the very criterion of their being sacred phenomena. An object of this kind is linked to a given local clan, because its spirit home lies within the area of this clan. Here the object materializes, i.e. the purely material form surrounding its inner core or *njäpan* is formed here by those members of the clan who stand in the right mythological relationship to the object, for they are the only persons able to make the genuine article. From here it is distributed to other territories, and when the material form is destroyed, its *njäpan* or spirit returns to its home. In this way the different clan areas become centres of production and distribution for special objects, which are spread far afield.

As early as in 1931 S. D. Porteus, the psychologist, pointed out that the people of Kimberley never imitated objects from other districts. When Porteus asked the Aborigines of Violet Valley why they did not make a special, hooked boomerang themselves, instead of importing it from other districts, they said that this form did not belong to their own area, and therefore they could not copy it.

From Kimberley we also have other information of interest in this connection. Thus, the Aborigines of this district are well-known for the serrated, small spear-heads which they make from crystal, agate, broken bottles, etc., and which they export from Kimberley to many parts of Northern Australia. J. R. B. Love, a missionary who has made a special study of the Worora tribe of this district, says that whenever one visits a Worora camp one will be almost certain to find someone busy making a spear-head of this particular type.

It seems unlikely that Love's account should be true of the whole Worora tribe; it is more likely that the above spear-heads are local totems of certain Worora clans, and that Love's account applies to these Worora clans only. Love claims that the mass production of the above spear-heads is a result of the enormous demand for such items among the Worora. But it seems more plausible that this tremendous production of spear-heads should be intended for the demonstrably extensive export to the Aborigines of other districts, who do not themselves produce them.

These spear-heads and the hooked boomerangs referred to above, as well as a number of other objects, are exported by way of ceremonial exchange cycles to Port Keats, and then farther towards the north-east to an untold number of people of different tribes. When these objects reach the Murinbata, they are regarded as being local totems of alien local clans. We might add that objects belonging to local clans living in the north-east and in the east of the Port Keats district also come to the Murinbata by way of ceremonial exchange cycles. But even though the Aborigines of Port Keats depend on many objects from the outside world, it should be emphasized that the greater, and by far the more important, part of the material equipment of the Murinbata is manufactured within the Port Keats district. And it is this production, or rather the distribution of the articles thus produced, with which we are here concerned.

To return to the sketch-map, p. 123. It appears from the map that a Murinbata will easily be able to contact all local groups within the circle, i.e. within his own tribal territory, and as will be shown below, these local groups together produce the most important of the utility articles used by the Murinbata. True, two Murinbata local clans, Maninj and Järere, have no artifacts among their local clan totems, but the other local clans of that tribe all include objects among their local totems. Thus, Wendek Nanaie has collecting bags, and Idiji has white pigment (used for body decoration) and a number of ceremonial spears among its local totems. Madjelindi has white and red pigment, string, and a special kind of rod (but not the prongs) for spearing fish. But the majority of objects are connected with Naŋu-Kultjil and Kurabäkal-Kultjil, whose clan areas all lie in the centre of the tribal territory. Thus, the local totems of Naŋu-Kultjil include paper-bark 'carry-all', ordinary spears, spear-throwers, clubs, and red pigment, while Kurabäkal-Kultjil have chanting tubes, beating sticks, fishing nets, digging sticks, and logs used as 'crafts'.

If we consider the objects that are manufactured within the Murinbata tribal territory more closely, and compare them with those which the Murinbata obtain from elsewhere by way of ceremonial exchange, certain differences appear clearly. Even though the Murinbata set great store by the textiles, mosquito nets, blankets, aluminium pans, steel axes and knives, etc., produced by the white man, they can manage without them. As for bull-roarers, hair belts, mother-of-pearl shells, boomerangs, shields, and other traditional objects which from time to time come to Port Keats from far-off clan areas, they are all of great significance to the Murinbata, and if the supply of these items ceased, the consequences would be serious. But in everyday life the Murinbata can manage without them too.

It should be mentioned that with the exception of bull-roarers, which all over Australia are regarded as sacred ceremonial items, the function of the other alien traditional objects may differ considerably from district to district. As these articles travel from the places where they were manufactured to the Port Keats district, the conception of their nature often changes on the way, so that the primary function of many objects becomes less important, or even loses all importance, while their secondary function is enhanced. As an example of this we may refer to the above-mentioned hooked boomerang from Kimberley. Among the people of Kimberley the main function of this boomerang is that of a missile, and it is constructed for this particular purpose. To the Murinbata, however, the primary function of the weapon is of practically no significance at all, and one hardly ever sees a Murinbata using such a boomerang as a missile. The secondary functions of this weapon have acquired the greatest significance among the Murinbata, to whom this boomerang is almost exclusively a ceremonial object for use during special ceremonies, and a status symbol for use on certain occasions.

Even though several of the traditional items which are imported to the Port Keats district may be of a certain 'practical' importance to the Murinbata, it should again be emphasized that their principle value to the Aborigines of this part of Australia lies in their use as objects of ceremony or status, or simply as items of personal adornment or as amulets.

But matters are entirely different as concerns those traditional objects which are manufactured within the Murinbata tribal territory. True, most of these items also have certain ceremonial functions, but the principal function of the majority of them is one of practical use in everyday life. These objects are all important tools and weapons, which the Aborigines must have if they are to survive. Thus, the spears and spear-throwers which are essential for hunting large game such as kangaroo and wallaby are produced within the Murinbata tribal territory, as is also practically all the fishing gear they use: spears for catching fish, fishing nets, and also 'crafts' (tree-trunks). Moreover, all the implements used for food-gathering: digging sticks, collecting bags, and paper-bark 'carry-all' are also made here. In other words, the entire economy of the Aborigines is based on implements which are, with very few exceptions, available within the Murinbata tribal territory. Furthermore, the spears and clubs most commonly used during the frequent fights between the Aborigines are also manufactured here. Finally it should be emphasized that the basic equipment required for all important ceremonies, i.e. musical instruments and red and white earth for decorating the body, is of Murinbata origin. It may be added that some very special ceremonial spears, used during a number of different ceremonies, are also produced within the Murinbata territory.

There are, however, some important utility articles, first and foremost fire-sticks for making a fire, which are not included among the Murinbata local clan totems. But normally a fire is lit from another fire, and as a rule there will always be a fire burning in some Murinbata camp or other. Moreover, fire-sticks are a local totem of the Marijädi local clan, Iljilijen, which lies only very little farther north of Port Keats than Madjelindi lies to the south. And thus the Murinbata will experience no difficulty in meeting their requirements for fire-sticks.

But even though the utility articles produced within the Murinbata territory do not fully cover the needs of the Murinbata, the Murinbata tribe as such may be said to be self-supporting as regards the essential equipment for food-gathering, fishing, hunting and fighting, and to some extent also for ceremonies. In other words, people living within the tribal territory will not need to communicate with those living elsewhere in order to cover their own requirements of the most important tools, weapons and other objects. The people of Maninj, for instance, who produce no artifacts at all, will turn to Wendek Nanaie for collecting bags, to Madjelindi for rods, to Kultjil-Naŋu for spear-throwers, etc.

Sometimes local clans that do not belong to the Murinbata tribe may also come to Madjelindi for rods, to Kultjil-Naŋu for spear-throwers, etc. But as all the objects manufactured within the Murinbata territory are also made elsewhere outside that region, it is normally not expedient for people of alien tribes to come to the Murinbata territory for articles that they can more easily obtain elsewhere. The point is that the Aborigines will, normally, contact the nearest centre of production of the goods required.

In 'Trade' in Aboriginal Australia, and 'Trade' Relationships with Torres Strait, New Guinea and Malaya, F. D. McCarthy points out that the way in which objects are handed over or exchanged may vary considerably among the Aborigines of Australia (McCarthy 1939: 177 ff.). In Kin and Totem I accounted for a particular exchange system by which a number of objects are passed on from person to person in the Port Keats district (Falkenberg 1962: 142 ff.). It should merely be added that the ceremonial exchange system referred to as *kulu* in *Kin and Totem* forms part of great ceremonial exchange cycles, which follow certain definite routes. A number of different objects are sent along these routes from tribe to tribe, and are thus distributed over vast regions. The above-mentioned hooked boomerangs and the special spear-heads of agate, crystal, and broken bottles, which come from Kimberley to Port Keats and are passed on to tribes in the north, are examples of objects distributed by means of *kulu* contacts.

The objects which are local totems in the Port Keats district are also occasionally sent in *kulu,* but we are at present concerned not with the extensive *kulu* contacts, but with the restricted distribution of objects within the Murinbata territory. As these objects, like so much else, are distributed (most commonly indirectly) on the basis of a *do ut des* principle, one may well ask what the people of the Murinbata clans Maninj and Järere, who include no objects among their local totems, are able to give in exchange for all those things which they themselves acquire from other local clans, and what form the distribution of objects to them takes. The answer is that the distribution of objects is merely part of a greater system of distribution, governing the exchange of services, rights, benefits as well as of objects. We saw above that the Aborigines classify their objects together with headaches, blood, animals, fish, birds, celestial bodies, etc. as local totems. Even though Järere and Maninj have no artifacts among their local totems, Maninj has over 20, and Järere more than 30 other local totems, which may well be as important to the Aborigines as objects. Thus, members of the Maninj clan or of the Järere clan may receive objects from other local clans and make return gifts by means of different services.

It should be noted that the exchange of objects, services, etc. which we have been discussing, is not a regular barter in which one commodity or service is balanced against another. Moreover, the reciprocal gift, or service, is not rendered on the spot, but may be deferred indefinitely. The point is that we are dealing with a totemic exchange system in which the ideas of value and property cannot be explained against a material, economic background.

I venture to conclude that all the hundreds of local totems which are distributed among the various local clans within the Port Keats district have led to extensive communication among the Aborigines, and that this communication has resulted in the establishment and maintenance of the

135

various tribes in this part of Australia. This contention is here illustrated by means of examples taken from one tribe, the Murinbata, and by one single category of local clan totems, i.e. material objects. It should, however, again be emphasized that an Australian tribe can be established as a result of a special geographical distribution of any categories of local clan totem. But if this is to happen, a limited area must possess a number of local clan totems of such a variety and of such great general importance that they, together, will lead to extensive communication between the people of the area in question.

As a final remark it should be added that the very structure of a local clan can easily lead to its isolation. Therefore, it seems reasonable to assume that an important reason for the production and distribution of sacred objects may well be that which also underlies the phenomenon of clan exogamy, namely a general need to establish contact with the outside world.

When the Port Keats mission station was founded in 1935, and the Aborigines from the entire district gathered there at regular, short intervals, stronger contacts were established not only between the Aborigines and the white man, but also between the Aborigines themselves. It is true that even before 1935 two or more hordes in the Port Keats district were periodically fused into larger local entities. But these gatherings did not take place as frequently as the large congregations around the mission station. Since members of a number of different local clans and tribes, from 1935 on, periodically lived together in one camp near the mission station, the need for more contact between the Aborigines was greatly reduced, and thus the very basis for the production and distribution of sacred objects disappeared. The disintegration of the Murinbata tribe was proceeding with gathering speed.

Bibliography

Falkenberg, J.
  1962 Kin and Totem. Oslo.
McCarthy, F. D.
  1939 'Trade' in Aboriginal Australia, and 'Trade' Relationships with Torres Strait, New Guinea and Malaya. Oscania X.
Thomson, D. F.
  1949 Economic Structure and the Ceremonial Exchange Cycle in Arnhem Land. Melbourne.

V
Art, Religion and Folklore

The spiritual life of the hunters echoes their environment, their life as hunters, and the society and values associated with this existence. The artistic creations of Palaeolithic hunters have amazed us for a long time. The same skill confronts us in later hunting art, in rock drawings and rock paintings, for example. Povl Simonsen's presentation of the rock art in the Tromsø region also mediates the symbolic functions of this art. There is no doubt that through the centuries the rock drawings of the huntsmen have conveyed religious and magical messages related to the game and its pursuit.

Two papers bear more directly on religious topics. Louise Bäckman analyses the ways in which the female perspective was represented in the northern Eurasian hunting religions: the woman as a goddess and as an unclean person. She correlates these traits with the social situation of the woman in the hunting society. Åke Hultkrantz discusses the intricate relations between the hunter's feeling for Nature and his religion, as exemplified by the Ojibway Indians in North America.

Hunting beliefs and attitudes have survived up till our own time and have even had influence upon recent methods of hunting. This is well brought out in Haraldur Ólafsson's paper on the hunter and the animal in modern Icelandic folklore. The past and the present have here come together in a synthesis. If we want proof of the survival of man's oldest traditional culture in a present-day milieu, here it is.

The Rock Art of the Huntsman in Troms

*Povl Simonsen**

Archaeological material in general was formerly looked upon from a diffusionistic point of view, as was rock art. But before the second World War another view had become predominant, according to which rock art was an expression of mentality, changing according to the social and economic conditions of the population. So art may be alike, and development may be parallel at many places on earth without any contact in the actual period. The most obvious manifestations of different mentality create two main groups of rock art (Hagen 1976, Simonsen 1979: 438–487): i.e. that of the farming people, and that of the hunters and fishers. The huntsman's art is described as physioplastic (Broby-Johansen 1944: 8–22):

It depicts the real, physical surroundings in the shape of naturalistic animal figures and now and then naturalistic human figures, the sense of which is to be found in the depicted phenomenon itself. The physioplastic, therefore, is in its origin pure naturalism, often in a simplified shape: outlined figures, strict profiles, natural size, etc. The peasant's art, on the contrary, is called ideoplastic, because it often expresses itself in symbols and abstractions: patterns, borders, heavily stylized figures, geometrical symbols, but also figures traditionally meaning something quite different from what they depict. For instance a boat picture may not only be so stylized that you cannot recognize the real boat, but at the same time it does not symbolize a boat or the sea, but the fertility of the fields!

The rock carvings of North Norway are physioplastic hunter's art (Gjessing 1932, Simonsen 1958, Hallström 1936). This art is looked upon as an integral part of the magic functions. Some of the scenes have been taken directly from the magic ceremonies themselves: dancing people, men beating the drum, etc. In accordance with the conceptions of the huntsman or the fisherman and with their magic needs, and also in accordance with the motives associated with the localities, we are able to conclude that the pictures have served as hunting magic, fishing magic, fertility magic to the wild beasts as well as to the people. Perhaps the ceremonies also aimed at success in love affairs, or the purpose has been

139

to help the medicine man in his work. We consider Stone Age religion shamanistic, the tasks of priest, sorcerer, and medicine man being united in one and the same person. Because of the aim of the art the figures normally have to be seen singly. Compositions are immensely rare, but they exist and prove the ability of the artist to express himself in this way, although it was not the custom to do so for magic purposes.

One problem which perhaps will never be fully solved is whether the single rock carving figure extended to repeated use, or whether its value only existed at the very moment of its creation. New and still more new figures were often made on the same tiny rock surface. This must indicate a conception of the spot as the home of some 'manes' or power. The place may have been loaded with power because of the existence of older figures there. But also the creation of the first figure on the rock must have had a reason. The power may have originated in some important event having taken place there: a child being born, a buck being killed, the sun-rays illuminating the place on some calendric occasion. But at the same time the repeated use of the rock often destroyed the old pictures, thus showing us the value of the picture at the creative moment, but not later on.

Only the older pictures, however, are fully physioplastic. They are naturalistic, outlined, full-sized figures, all of them representing wild animals. Gradually the animals get more or less stylized, the size is diminished, and the interior of the body is filled out with details of different types. At the same time the spectrum of motifs is widened to human figures, implements, structures, even geometrical signs of an abstract content, which we are seldom able to understand. Thus many ideoplastic elements are developed. In spite of this one should always speak of a stylized physioplastic, never of an ideoplastic art. It has been discussed why this change from early naturalism to later stylization took place. Gutorm Gjessing (1945: 293) advanced the following, very likely, hypothesis: Right up until the middle of the Late Stone Age – ca. 2000–1500 B.C. – the hunting magic, and as a consequence of this the art had been the work of an individual huntsman, but at this time the magic became professionalized by the first generation of full-time shamans. The relation between the shaman and the art was not the same as between the huntsman and the art, and the growing distance between the artist and hunting life caused an alteration in style and a growing need for symbols, depicting those human wishes of which you cannot make a true picture: fertility in general, warmth, rain, peace etc. As an example I shall mention a certain geometric figure sometimes to be found inside a rhombic frame, sometimes as filling out the body of a female figure. We think that the former example represents fertility as an abstraction, while the latter marks out the human figure as female to the spectators and to the supernatural powers. In fact, it is not strange that the professional shaman should appear on the stage at this time (Simonsen 1975). The professional tradesman had already existed for centuries, and at this juncture we also meet the potter and the mason.

Obviously art and ritual, connected with special aims and special, power-loaded localities, is not to be found just anywhere in the landscape. A map of the rock-carving localities and an analysis of their micro-environment tell us a great deal about the hunting/fishing and about the society. The localities are intimately connected either to the shore-line or to running water, not only as an expression of the customs of people and prey, but so closely that it must have had a particular meaning. They are often placed on the migration routes of the wild reindeer or at their swimming places when crossing the sounds. Or they may be exactly where you will still today find the best fishing places. Now and then the Stone Age dwelling site is next to a rock carving, but often the locality is a good hunting or fishing place far from the dwelling site. The rock used for making pictures may be vertical or oblique, exposed to south or east, but in other cases it is a dome-shaped rock, the oldest of the pictures being at the highest point. The motifs tell us about animals being hunted and eaten: moose, reindeer, bear, goose, dolphin, halibut, and salmon, more seldom hare, cormorant, etc. We also learn about the hunting and fishing methods. The hunter disguises himself as an animal with antlers or long ears; the use of a hound is a part of the hunting technique; the fisherman uses a long line with a stone sinker at the lower end; the hunter uses spear or bow-and-arrow; moose and reindeer are captured in pitfalls; the reindeer are hunted while swimming the sound just in front of the rock carving. Men use skis or row small boats. All this must be traces of hunting and fishing magic. But there are also representations of copulating human beings, of extremely phallic men, likewise of moose, of pregnant women, and in one case an 'x-ray photo' of a pregnant whale. Here we presume fertility magic. Next we have the dancing and drumming scenes, depicting the magic ceremonies themselves. Finally we meet such symbols as must be imported from Southern Scandinavia, and the naturalistic background of which must have been intelligible to arctic man. The snake as a symbol appears hundreds of kilometres farther north than any living snake; the cart-wheel – perhaps being a sun-symbol – portrayed no reality to Scandinavian people, except in the extreme south. In this way we notice migrating conceptions and motifs in the magic-religious world on the rock surfaces.

All the traits I have mentioned are to be found at these few localities, existing in the neighbourhood of Tromsø (Simonsen 1955). Still more traits and a still better impression of the everyday life and the magic conceptions of Stone Age hunters are at our disposal if we include such wide larger rock carving localities as Alta in Finnmark (investigated by Knut Helskog, but still unpublished), Nämforsen in Ångermanland (Hallström 1960), and the beaches of the White Sea and Lake Onega (Ravdonikas 1936–38, Savvateev 1967).

Notes

* During the NRAF-symposium in Tromsø the author gave a general survey of the North-Scandinavian rock art and its problems, and on the excursion acted as guide at the following rock art localities: Kirkely, Gråbergan, and Bukkhammaren in Balsfjord commune, Skavberg I and III in Tromsø commune. Here only those parts of the lectures directly related to the theme of the symposium, the huntsman's existence and conceptions, will be published.

Bibliography

Broby-Johansen, R.
  1944 Hverdagskunst – Verdenskunst. Copenhagen.
Gjessing, G.
  1932 Arktiske helleristninger i Nord-Norge. Oslo.
  1945 Norges steinalder. Oslo.
Hagen, A.
  1976 Bergkunst. Oslo.
Hallström, G.
  1936 Monumental Art of Northern Scandinavia. Stockholm.
  1960 Monumental Art of Northern Sweden from the Stone Age. Stockholm.
Ravdonikas, B. J.
  1936–38 Naskal'nye isobratschenija Onetschkogo Ozero i Belogo Morja. 2 volumes. Leningrad.
Savvateev, J. A.
  1967 Risunki na skalach. Petrozavodsk.
Simonsen, P.
  1955 Helleristninger ved Tromsø. Ottar 5.
  1958 Arktiske Helleristninger i Nord-Norge II. Oslo.
  1975 When and why did Occupational Specialization Begin at the Scandinavian North Coast? Pp. 75–86 in Prehistoric Maritime Adaptations of the Circumpolar Zone. The Hague.
  1979 Veidemenn på Nordkalotten. Oslo.

Female – Divine and Human

A study of the Position of the Woman in Religion and Society in Northern Eurasia

Louise Bäckman

We will here, from the point of view of Saami society, attempt to throw some light upon the situation of women, that is, their role on the mythological, religious and social levels, in North Eurasian society. However, it is not at all our intention to seek to demarcate a sharp boundary between male and female and thereby demonstrate an irreconcilable polarity. The masculine and the feminine are aspects of the same phenomenon – life itself – and, as the one is dependent upon the other, the two can never be separated; this is a truism, but one that must be pointed out. The generalizations in the article are due to limitations of space and, moreover, we must remain aware of the possibilities of variations in the shaping of a society's structure and also that the conditions of all the societies in the area concerned have changed a lot during the last half century.

The gender of the terminology already points to a dichotomy in man's ideas about the world of the gods, wherein we find both male and female divinities active in different functional areas. The goddess as a rule stands in an intimate proximity to man: birth, sustenance, and death all lie within her sphere, and in many cases animals too are protected by female divinities. The god as a rule stands outside this circle of intimacy; the boundaries of his power are wider and more overlapping. In the eighteenth-century sources for the southern Saami region a number of fragments of a myth have been found which, when assembled, form a narrative relating how a person is created. Its content is, essentially, that life emanates from a celestial male deity and that three female deities, closely bound to the mortal world, serve as mediators. Man is then, according to this myth, both a celestial and a worldly creature. The three goddesses actively participate in the process of creation; the Ur-mother, *Madder-akka,* creates the body enveloping the 'soul', which she obtains

143

from the god, while her daughters *Sarakka* and *Juksakka* produce the sex of the child. These goddesses along with a third daughter, *Ugsakka,* function as tutelary beings for the woman and her child, and one of them, *Sarakka,* is also referred to as the protectress of the husband and the home in general. She dwells in the hearth, and every day food and drink are offered to her there. *Madder-akka* and *Sarakka* also promote fertility in animals, and newborn reindeer calves are under their protection. (The names of the daughters vary in the accounts of different authors but the content of the myth remains the same.) (Kildal 1945: 135, 143, Skanke 1945: 184 f. See also Reuterskiöld 1910: 57 f.). There are also accounts which indicate that *Sarakka* once took part in the creation of the world (Högström 1980: 184).

Also among the Russian Saami we can trace notions about a 'Birth-Mother' who, like *Madder-akka* and her daughter *Sarakka,* aided women during childbirth. Her name was *Sjant-aik* and, according to the vague information we have concerning her, she was also considered to be the 'Mother of God'. She has probably borrowed some of her features from Christian notions but, writes Genetz, her name could be derived from a verb which corresponds to 'hervorbringen' (Genetz 1891: XXXIX). The Saamis in Finland also spoke about a deity with the name of *Madder-ahkku,* but her functions were other ones than those mentioned above: she gave back hearing to the deaf and sight to the blind and helped those gone astray to find the right way. Offerings were made to her at certain places outside the home, in contrast to the Saami customs in the west. The name, however, indicates a close connection with the West Saami Ur-mother/Clan-mother as the first of the elements in her name, *madder-,* is derived from a word denoting 'root', 'origin', 'earth', and her concern was centred about the individual.

The antipode of life – death – is also ruled by a female being, *Jabme-akka,* the Death-hag (or Death-goddess). She was as important as the Ur-mother herself and can perhaps be understood as an aspect of her. Men were conscious of *Jabme-akka,* but she does not seem to have been the object of any cult in daily life; she was the divine ruler over a region that was so remote and so shadowy that no special attention was given her except on certain special occasions, such as when she was propitiated with sacrifices in order to help a kinsman regain his health. In her capacity as ruler over the kingdom of the dead, she also determined the length of an individual's life (see for example Kildal 1945: 139 f.).

In the Saami mythology there is also another female divinity with a definite fertility aspect, *Rana-nieide,* who ruled over the mountain meadows and made them turn green at the right time. Her exact nature is difficult to determine, and she has sometimes been considered a figure borrowed from agrarian cultures and thus not to have belonged to the original hunter's religion (Kildal 1945: 142. Harva in manuscript 1915: 101). However, it is not impossible that she belongs to the North Eurasian pantheon as well, since we find a counterpart to her function in other mythologies concerned.

Concerning the *akka*s, which among the western Saamis were involved with the act of birth, researchers are generally in agreement that *Madder-akka* is a part of the North Eurasian pantheon and as such an archaic element in the Saami religion. She is the Earth-Mother whose prototype can be found in the Middle-Eastern Magna Mater figure, as Lid tells us (Lid 1946: 20), and Nahodil says that her origin has to be sought at the very dawn of religion, since she represents the Ur-mother for both animals and human beings (Nahodil 1963: 492, 508). The Great Mother acts as capriciously as nature itself, notes Neumann, she is a life-affirming power, but simultaneously she has death in her hand, and the attitude towards her was characterized by a certain ambivalence. The origin of the daughters of *Madder-akka,* whose functions seems to be aspects of the Ur-mother herself, has, on the other hand, proved to be more difficult to determine. They display surprising similarities with the Scandinavian *norns,* who determined a person's fate and who were also thought to aid a woman during childbirth (Lid 1946: 19, Grundström 1956: 205, note 2). They also show similarities with those kinds of 'domestic spirits' called among other things 'bolvättar', which are represented in the Scandinavian folk tradition. Because of this they have also been interpreted as being a loan from the Scandinavians, who were the closest western neighbours of the Saamis. Ränk, however, has shown that these daughters of *Madder-akka* also belong to the cultural type of North Eurasia. In his opinion all the four *akka*s belong to the 'house-' or 'clan-spirits' that a newly married Siberian woman used to bring with her from her parents' home to her husband's dwelling-place. The 'clan-gods' a woman took with her, like the western Saami *akka*s, helped and protected her above all during menstruation, pregnancy, and childbirth. These deities, which belonged to the gods of her own clan, were, as Ränk sees it, as such originally ancestral spirits, and he also believes that *Madder-akka* and her daughters originally constituted a group of the souls of the dead, 'as is the case with all the subterranean deities' (Ränk 1955: 77). We can, however, look upon the *akka*s from another point of view, and later on we will return to the subject.

Among the Saamis in the West as well as among those in the East, not only humans but animals too possessed supernatural protectors, and the tutelary spirits of several kinds of animals were imagined as possessing female characteristics. Thus migratory birds were watched over by 'mothers', *Barbmo-akka,* in the belief of the western Saamis, or *Loddisj-äd'ne,* which is also known in the eastern area. It was also a female spirit, *Luohtt-hosjek,* who protected the wild reindeer in the belief of the Skolt-Saamis (Itkonen 1946: 78 f.) to give but a few examples.

In the mythologies of the other peoples of North Eurasia we find that the female element is well-entrenched, despite the ceremonial 'uncleanliness' of the mortal woman, a question to which we will return. Nahodil (1963) and Simčenko (1978) point to the widespread belief among these peoples of 'mother'-figures, which dominate their pantheons. These 'mothers' are responsible for natural phenomena and for the welfare of animals and humans. The most prominent of these 'mothers' is the *Giver of life* and *Protectress of women and children* who, like *Madder-akka* and her daughters, actively takes part in the birth-process. All fertility, that of man as well as of animals, was dependent upon her and among many peoples she bears names reminiscent of Mother Earth or All-Mother. An equally important feminine being is Mother Fire, who is appealed to as the protectress of the material welfare of the home, the family, and the clan. Often the two goddesses merge into one another in the ideas of the peoples and also into 'female spirits' with other duties, as Nahodil and Simčenko point out. Mother Fire, like *Sarakka* among the Saamis, had her cult-place in the hearth; both were daily given portions of food and drink, and both of them were the dominant beings of the home: among the Nganasan, Simčenko says for example, '... the cult of *Tu-njami,* Mother Fire, occupied an exclusive place [...] Mother Fire protected the home, assisted in childbirth, chased off diseases, purified people who violated some sacred establishment' (Simčenko 1978: 510). *Sarakka,* in her place, was the most beloved of all divinities according to the sources ('she is the most dear and the most dependable of all the beings which they hold themselves to' Skanke 1945: 189). A Saami woman prayed to her for a good birth, and when a child fell ill it was re-named with a ceremony of baptism, which was performed 'in the name of *Sarakka',* so that the child would recover (Reuterskiöld 1910: 3). Before they took Holy Communion – which they were forced to do – the Saamis performed rites similar to it in *Sarakka*'s honour 'and pray to *Sarakka* for forgiveness that they are now compelled to go to *Ibmelgare,'* [meaning God's bowl or dish, i.e. Holy Communion] (Reuterskiöld 1910: 3).

Here we can only point out that the worship of and reliance on supernatural female beings has been widespread and common and as important as the worship of male divinities, though the latter seem to have been more removed from the daily needs of man; we cannot, however, with certainty maintain that myth and cult reflect the social order. Still Nahodil and with him Simčenko and others hold that the well-documented female element in myth and cult is proof of an original matriarchal social order among all peoples, not merely the agrarians. 'Im Gegenteil, das Matriarchat ist die älteste und die allgemeinste Form der Sippenorganisation der Gesellschaft, die sogar bei den Jägern der sibirischen Taiga, den sibirischen Renzüchtern und Seefischern bestand' (Nahodil 1963: 507). The question of matriarchy will not be discussed any further here,[1] but the theory that the cult of the goddess was forced to yield to that of the god as the social order changed from matriarchal into patriarchal, as Nahodil and others believe, has to be dismissed as speculative, as Jettmar quite justifiably maintains. We can, however, say that there was a state of balance between the masculine and feminine: 'In Wirklichkeit dürfte hier ein alter Gleichgewichtszustand, eine säuberliche Teilung der Kompetenzen vorliegen' (Jettmar 1954: 24).

According to Nahodil, the existence of a matriarchy as the first and original social order is further confirmed by the archaeological finds made over a broad belt extending from central Siberia in the East (that is, not in the tundra zone) to northwest Europe in the West. The finds most pertinent here are the so-called Venus statuettes, the finding places of which are connected with the dwelling places of primitive agrarians and hunters, where the women had their working areas and where the dead were buried. The time span of the statuettes covers a period of many thousands of years, for they can be dated back through prehistoric times all the way to the paleolithic. Various theories about the function of these statuettes have been put forward; apart from the assumption that they portray the 'erotic ideal Venus', the majority of researchers believe that the figures symbolize a supernatural activity. Some consider them as amulettes, that is, magical guarantors of fertility, while others hold them to be symbols of divine beings like the Ancestral-mother, the Mother-goddess, the Fertility-goddess, the Mistress of animals, etc. Maringer, however, sees them as representatives of the practitioners of cultic practices, that is, worshippers and priestesses, as well as the objects of the cult practices, that is, divine beings. The woman in prehistoric times appeared in a double religious role. In her passive role she was the embodiment of the 'weiblicher Gottheiten' and in her active one 'Offizianten in magisch-religiösen Kulten' (Maringer 1979: 767, see also Maringer 1977: 101 f.). We can with confidence assume that the field of the statuettes' activity was centred around the daily life of the family, and birth and death, and consequently we can say that they are symbols for the protectress of the family, of the hearth and home, and of material welfare in general.

In a society in which hunting is a prerequisite for survival itself, it is obvious that everyone, regardless of sex, shares the burden of work, and that the division of labour is made upon a practical basis. In general it can be said that the man, being physically stronger, is the producer, i.e. he procures the basic foodstuffs and represents the group for which he has responsibility, as a rule a nuclear family, to the outside world. The area of his activity has a broad base. The woman in her turn is the reproducer, i.e. she gives birth to and rears children and takes care of the necessary maintenance of house and home. On her shoulders, at least when the family is nomadic, rests the entire responsibility for the management of the dwelling-place, and it is also her task to provide for the material needs of the family in a practical manner as, for example, to prepare the meals and manufacture clothing – the last is something especially important for a hunter in an arctic or subarctic climate. She also contributes to their provisions by gathering the vegetable foods in season, and it is often also her task to supply the family with fish from lakes. She also has a part in the economic management of the household, since she is often the one who controls the family's food supplies. In contrast to the man, her range of work is spatially more circumscribed, since her tasks are tied to the home or the dwelling-place.

The division of labour is made from the male/female aspect or, if one will, it is the natural one, and the individual begins to learn the various facets of his labour at an early age. Among the Nenetz, for example, the father takes over the education of his sons when they reach the age of six or seven and teaches them hunting, fishing, and reindeer-herding, while his daughters remain at their mother's side to be trained in their own future duties (Levin/Potapov 1964: 564). Not only the techniques of labour are acquired but the art of interpreting the changes in nature and of the seasons – a skill necessary for the survival of the group – is learned as well.[2] An important part of an individual's identity is his access to the cultural heritage of his group; this includes the traditional stories and myths, the learning of which has to be begun at a very early age. Among the Saamis the herding of reindeer and the occupations connected with it were mastered by means of observations and participation from early childhood; children had personal responsibility for the tasks they were entrusted with. Here there was a strict natural division of labour as well: the man took all responsibility for the reindeer herd while the woman assumed that for the home. During migrations her duties included the setting up of the tent, the collection of firewood, and packing and unpacking. She also oversaw the family's economy by planning for the replacement of supplies and in later times by making the necessary purchases and the like. Reindeer herding, however, demands teamwork and when needed the wife stepped in to help her husband as, for example, when an extra guard was needed for the reindeer herd or at the times of milking, calf branding or slaughtering. Similar duties can be noted among other nomadic peoples in northern Siberia (Levin/Potapov 1964: 646 concerning the Evenk). According to an investigation undertaken in 1978 at the Saami Institu'tta, Kautokeino, this relationship has not noticeably changed among the reindeer-rearing Saamis of Finnmark, in northern Norway. There women still have a strong position in the family as well as in the group, even if they still do not represent the family to the outside world to any great degree; that is, they do not participate in decisions concerning problems common to the village (Dieðot 1979, No. 4).

Differences between the sexes were not restricted to the practical level but were found on the intellectual one as well. Traditional stories possessed by the group seem to follow different patterns both in terms of their content and their method of presentation depending on the sex of the reciter. Further differences can be observed in other areas: Among the Nanay for example a woman was not allowed to sing – this was a male prerogative – and among the Chukchi differences between male and female pronunciation were distinguished (Levin/Potapov 1964: 710, 800), a phenomenon that can also be observed among other peoples all over the world. That the significance of this differentiation was strictly maintained can be seen in the fact that a transvestite – for instance a man who had assumed a female role and who also served as a shaman – would not only appropriate the occupational role and demeanour of a woman but her speech patterns as well. According to ethnological literature, the Chukchi are one of the peoples who accepted transvestism as a social privilege (see Baumann 1955: 16 f. where he refers to Bogoras).[3]

On the cultic plane sex differences were expressed in taboo notions among the Saamis as well as among other groups in North Eurasia. Places of sacrifice were forbidden to the Saami woman, that is, she was not allowed to enter them or even to approach them. Moreover, certain sacrificial acts were reserved for men only and so was the use of the shaman's drum. These ceremonial prohibitions, which were applied to her as long as she was capable of childbearing, she shared with women of other cultures. According to the Finnish tradition, a woman was forced to make long, time-consuming, detours to avoid places considered holy, and both the Finnish and the Saami woman was forbidden to fish in lakes held to be holy (in Fi. *pyhä,* in Saa. *passe/bâsse/bissie*). Similar religious taboos were also found among other Finno-Ugric speaking peoples such as the Manshi or Shanti (see Vilkuna 1956 and Kannisto 1958). But there are exceptions from these taboo-rules: the Chukchi woman performed without restrictions her part of the rites of the great sacrificial ceremonies which took place in the autumn and spring when the seasons changed (Levin/Potapov 1964: 822). There were also varieties in the prohibitions: e.g. a woman among the Enetz, a Samoyed group, could handle a shaman drum, whereas among the Saamis, as mentioned, a woman was not even allowed to be seen in the vicinity of one or travel in the tracks left when a drum had been transported. The Enetz woman consequently could become a shaman of the highest rank (Prokofyeva 1963) while a Saami woman apparently had to content herself with acting as one of the lower rank (Bäckman/Hultkrantz 1978). According to Gustav Ränk, the taboos, where they are to be found, only applied to a woman who had *married* into the group, but apparently among most peoples concerned they were applied to all women capable of bearing children even if the rules could vary. Rombandjejewa noticed with certainty that a Manshi woman had to alter her behaviour at her first menstruation (Rombandjejewa 1963: 85).

Still, in the notions of the religious taboo there was a certain ambivalence: on the one hand, a holy area was dangerous for a woman and could bring about sickness or some other evil for her and, on the other hand, she herself was considered 'unclean' and as such was herself dangerous. Thus a woman was just as 'dangerous' for her surroundings, above all for men but also for the places concerned, as the sanctity of a holy place was for her. As women had the capacity to give birth and to menstruate, they were surrounded by 'mysterious, dangerous powers', as Heiler expresses it (Heiler 1977: 9).[4] These 'powers' were in the popular conception, according to the ethnological literature, considered as being 'unclean' and harmful to a man, his hunting equipment and his weapons and to superhuman powers. The most dangerous times were during pregnancy, childbirth, and menstruation, when a woman was forced to isolate herself from places frequented by men or to mark her condition by, for example, a special detail in her clothing such as not wearing a belt as the custom was among the Saamis. In this turn a man could not participate in the rites devoted to female deities that were considered the special tutelary spirits for women, such as the above-mentioned 'clan-spirits'; nor could he touch any images a woman might have or stay in the place in the dwelling where these were kept without suffering adverse consequences.[5]

The sacred images were very dangerous for him, but to claim therefore that these female tutelary deities were in themselves 'unclean' as Lehtisalo does (Lehtisalo 1924: 111) is to draw much too far-ranging conclusions about antagonisms between men and women. In my opinion the conceptions of 'danger' were reciprocal: a woman had to be careful about certain places and actions while a man had to be careful about others.[6]

In general in the North Eurasian cultures – with some exceptions – the woman is believed to have had a position in the family subordinate to that of the man. The 'bride-price', 'bride-stealing', and the inability to inherit, as well as patrilocal residence, have been taken as indications that in various cultures the women were not officially considered full members of their communities but as the property of males and as legitimate objects for their arbitrariness. To this can be added such phenomena as polygamy, wife-exchange, and 'hospitality prostitution', all of which ethnographic terms have a negative connotation for us, which can occasionally be reduced to 'interpretations' of observations.

Kai Donner, writing about Samoyed in general (here probably Selkup), says that the woman's position among them was a very low one; she was 'a necessary and useful labourer' and was besides considered 'the property of a man in the same way as a reindeer or a dog'. 'He can never win her as a wife through love', he continues, 'as is the most usual case amongst us, but solely through purchase' (Donner 1915: 69). Castrén, another of the earlier writers, made the same observations amongst the Ostyak (Shanti) and among all 'the savages in Siberia' (Castrén 1870: 310 ff.). 'Amongst the Ostyak still the woman is estimated and treated like the most worthless slave', and he continues that nothing else could be worse 'than the shabby business the Ostyak practise with their daughters' (Castrén 1855: 56 f.), referring to the custom of 'bride-price'. However, in a description of the customs of the Nenetz, another Samoyed group, Prokofyera, a later Soviet ethnographer, writes that the woman had a high status in the family and '. . . the wife's opinion carried great weight and was always taken into account' (Levin/Potapov 1964: 564). Here we should recall that the 'bride-price' was important among the Nenetz, and that a woman was considered ceremonially 'unclean' and could not inherit (Levin/Potapov 1964: 564 f.). Unfortunately, because of limitations of space, we cannot discuss in greater detail the concepts mentioned above, but the greatest likelihood is that they were judged, in many cases, according to different criteria, depending on the point of view of the person making the judgement. In every group, regardless of the type of society to which it may belong, there are unspoken rules about how the individual is to behave in various situations, rules that are acquired intuitively through affiliation to a group and the codes of which can only be interpreted by members of that group. The rules give security and create a feeling of identity. It can be difficult for an outsider to judge any given situation in a satisfactory manner, since he or she is bound by his own frames of reference and has his own interpretational codes. Eric Solem, who is of the opinion that among the Saamis women enjoyed a high and respected position, once expressed his surprise that they shouldered such a great burden of work without complaint while men had a much lighter one. A woman, according to Solem, had to assume complete responsibility for all the tasks carried out in the home. The men confirmed Solem's supposition but this, he was told, was because the woman 'was so able and trustworthy' (Solem 1933: 64). Naturally this was only a part of the truth; both sexes carried out their respective traditional roles. Skanke, one of the source-writers, however, sees the division of labour between men and women as unjust and a means for oppressing women (Skanke 1945: 219 f.). Von Westen, another source-writer from the same area, expresses himself differently: he lists the 'delusions of the Finns' [Saamis] under 23 headings and heading number 16 reads: 'The dominion and tyranny of the women over their husbands' (Reuterskiöld 1910: 109).

In the Saami society and the others treated here, marriage was a concern of the family/clan of the contracting parties, and the young couples had to comply with the choice of their families. In the ceremonial courting it was always the family of the man that took the active role, and it would have been chiefly the woman from whom compliance was demanded. In certain families it was the mother of the woman who finally judged the suitability of the respective partners (Solem 1933: 115 on the Russian Saamis, Levin/Potapov 1964: 536 on the Manshi). In choosing a marriage partner consideration was usually paid to the future husband's or wife's economic prospects, that is it was the 'initial capital' of the marriage as well as the possibility of future support which were decisive. The lack of 'capital', however, could be offset by industriousness, a notion that was characteristic of the Saamis. 'Renlycka', 'luck with reindeer', is a term that often recurs in descriptions of the marriage customs of the Saamis, and we should not only understand it as referring to the number of reindeer which one of the partners brought into the marriage but his ability to handle a herd and to make use of its products. A partner who was poor in material possessions but capable could therefore be considered as a suitable prospective bride or groom.

'Bride-price' was common amongst most peoples; the husband's family, or sometimes clan, after careful negotiations presented gifts to the family or clan of the prospective bride. Had he not the means, the man could make up for the 'bride-price' by working in the woman's family during a set period of from one to three years, but occasionally there was both a 'bride-price' and a period of labour and Solem believes that the custom of working for the bride was the original one among the Saamis (Solem 1933: 153). It appears among most of the Siberian peoples and among the Chukchi it is universal (Levin/Potapov 1964: 152), among whom 'stealing' of the bride was also sanctioned.

As a rule it was the family or clan that received the gifts of the prospective groom. These could consist of money, other objects of value, cattle or reindeer. Among the Russian Saamis it was, however, the bride's parents who received the price (Solem 1933: 109 f., 115). When the marriage was an established fact, the dowry was handed over by the bride's parents, and among the Saamis this could correspond to the value of the 'bride-price'. The dowry chiefly consisted of items of utility to the bride: clothing and household utensils, as well as cattle and reindeer. The reindeer that a Saami bride brought with her formed the basis of her economic independence, since she had full rights over the herd that was built up with these animals (Solem 1933: 168). She could also make decisions that concerned the family, but she does not seem to have taken part, at least not officially, in the decision-making process of the group as a whole. We should probably consider the exchange of these valuables ('bride-price' and 'dowry') as a means of establishing important relations between two families rather than as payment for 'the loss of her [the bride's] valuable productive and reproductive services' (the 'bride-price') and a contribution 'to help cover the cost of maintaining an economically burdensome woman ...' (the dowry), as Harris wishes us to interpret the custom (Harris 1978: 59). Negotiations about the 'bride-price' show that it was not simply a matter of purchase; it also had another significance: a higher 'price' enhanced the status of the bride and her family or clan, and this in its turn affected her as well as her husband. Through a marriage one established new familial relations with their resultant obligations; this is shown by another custom found among the Saamis in the southern Saami area: the *la'kko*-institution. At a wedding it was customary for both the bride and the groom to 'buy' the right to address their respective parents-in-law by the *la'kko*-titles *father-* and *mother-in-law* (Kristoffer Sjulssons minnen 1979: 173).

Up to now we have been absorbing descriptions and analyses of customs and practices as given by researchers about peoples who were foreign to them. These have included linguists, ethnographers, ethnologists, anthropologists etc., but a common feature is that they were and are from cultures outside the field of their research. Now the various peoples they have been examining will speak for themselves, and we will quote Jurij Rytcheu, a well-known Soviet writer and journalist, who grew up in and is a part of the Chukchi milieu. Concerning the custom of 'working for the bride' he writes as follows: 'It could happen that a suitor was obliged to undergo certain tests. In this case he took up residence in his future father-in-law's hut and carried out miscellaneous chores in the home, brought home game, and, to be brief, did everything which was required of a married man. Sometimes the fiancée could even have children but this was not at all considered sufficient evidence that the husband-to-be had passed all the tests. After a few years it could appear that he was unsuitable in some respect and then his place was taken by another suitor. Those who "worked for" their fiancées in this way were as a rule men who had no household themselves to speak of and who hoped to establish familiar ties with a rich clan' (Rytcheu 1980).

Residence after marriage could be both patrilocal and matrilocal, at least that was the state of affairs among the Saamis, who also reckoned their families bilaterally. In strictly patrilocal clans it seems to have been principally the man's family that decided where the young couple would live. In cases where 'working for the bride' was established, the residence was automatically matrilocal for the time before the couple moved to their own dwelling.

'Hospitality prostitution', 'wife-exchange', and 'wife-lending' are terms that were established early by researchers with an occidental-Christian view of sexuality. By formulating the customs in these terms they could demonstrate that the people under discussion considered women as an item of trade and a possession with which one could act arbitrarily.

154

Without denying that customs differ from one culture to another, we must say that these are ethnographic terms that engender a negative attitude in our mind. In order to understand a phenomenon correctly we have to know the peoples' own designation for it and, moreover, all the connotations of the term, and we have to put the phenomenon into the cultural context where it belongs. The interpretation of the customs may then be quite different, and we can see that fortunately the approach is being modified more and more. In *Circumpolar peoples* we read concerning the customs of the Yukagir that: 'The young Yukagirs were sexually free before marriage. When a girl reached puberty she received her own sleeping tent in her father's dwelling and she was free to receive young men during the night, . . .'. And concerning 'hospitality prostitution' we see the following: 'The Yukagirs practised a form of what older ethnographers called "hospitality prostitution" (a bad term since no prostitution is involved), in which men visiting a Yukagir camp were offered the bed of a young girl for the night; the explanation was that it was the bed and not the girl that was offered to the visitor – the girl could do as she pleased. It must be noted that after a period of sexual experimentation many Yukagirs remained together as couples and faithfulness was a Yukagir ideal' (Graburn/Strong 1973: 46). The girl thus had the right to decide for herself, according to the article. (See also Kjellström 1973: 170 f. concerning the Eskimo.) We can also note what Rytcheu writes about 'wife-exchange' and 'wife-lending'. He does not deny sexual customs foreign to us but, in my view, he makes statements that are exaggeratedly moralistic but rational in a way: 'With sorrow in my heart I have come to read in a number of books of the reported custom of trading wives, or by expressions of hospitality when the newly-arrived guest of honour not only should have been given the best which the host can manage, but is offered a place in the marital bed as well. There are a number of stories about this. But the custom was actually strictly regulated and practised extremely seldom and only then "when it was really necessary». In this highly respectable custom there was not a trace of moral laxity or an attempt to enliven a dull marriage with novelty. Men lived in closed societies which were often separated from each other by vast wilderness of snow and ice. Under such circumstances the danger of inbreeding dictated the rules and forced people to renew their blood and inject new vigor into the community, clan and family. The chief concern in this custom was again the welfare of future generations and the health of people who not only had to exist, but to live often in a bitter struggle against a harsh and treacherous nature' (Rytcheu 1980: 9).

We cannot here closely examine the question of inheritance, which is a complicated issue, but a woman as a rule did not seem to have been left completely without a share; on the one hand, she received a dowry, which in some cases became her own property, and on the other hand was placed under the protection of her own familial gods in her new home, which was the case in some societies. The Saamis of Scandinavia followed the laws of inheritance of their respective countries: a son inherited two-thirds and a daughter one-third from their family (Drake 1918: 231). This was the case in Sweden until 1848, whereafter a son and a daughter were given equal rights. We do not know for sure how the inheritance was divided before the Saamis began herding reindeer and when their economy was still based on hunting and fishing, since there was then no accumulated property to be divided. It is interesting, however, writes Solem, that there seems to be traces of the 'right of inheritance of the youngest son' among the Saamis (Solem 1933: 169 f.). This phenomenon is represented among other Finno-Ugric peoples as well, with some exceptions, and among other groups of northern Siberia, as for instance amongst the Ket (Shimkin 1933: 157). The older children formed their own families and built their own homes while the youngest son remained behind at home with his parents and after his father's death he took over the house and the fire. He then usually had the responsibilities for his younger unmarried sisters as well as his mother as long as she lived. The fire was important; it was the symbol of the home's security; there the Fire-Mother had her seat, and among the Chukchi, and others, the fire itself was considered to be holy and was inherited from the father's side to the youngest son (Levin/Potapov 1964: 820). Probably the fire had a great significance for the Saamis as well. *Sarakka,* the special tutelary spirit of the woman, the home and the family, had, as previously stated, her dwelling place in the hearth and was daily offered food and drink there.

One's personal possessions, such as hunting equipment for a man and sewing materials for a woman, could not be appropriated by another after death as these followed the body into the grave to be used in the next life (see König 1929: 646, Shimkin 1939: 157), a custom that was practised among the Saamis as well. Real property, such as a dwelling with its effects, boats, and reindeer herds, was, on the other hand, the common property of the family. Among the Yakut and the Samoyed groups, König tells us, the economic security of a widow was dependent upon her sons, since she took over the real property and administered it for them in their minority (König 1929: 647). A childless widow, however, seems to have been deprived of any guarantee if she did not follow the Saami custom of returning to her own family. An Ostyak widow with her children, according to Castrén, was taken care of by a male relation of her late husband, but at the same time the Ostyak practised levirate, i.e. a young man had to marry his older brother's widow and accept the responsibility for her future (Castrén 1870: 312).

That the woman as a powerful supernatural being has a prominent place in the mythologies of these peoples while, as a community member she is subordinated, though not always oppressed, is a circumstance that appears to be contradictory. Nahodil and others seek to solve this problem by elaborating on Bachofen's (Das Mutterrecht 1861) theory that a matriarchy wherein a Mother Goddess was enthroned as the foremost and most important cult object and women and their families controlled the group, was the first organized society. Later society changed for various reasons, including economic ones, and when feudal rule became fully developed, men assumed political power and forced the women down to a secondary level. Simultaneously the cult changed. Prokofyeva (see Jettmar 1954: 24, where she is quoted) says for example that the Mother Goddess retired before the Sky God, who became the leading cult object in this world of men. In the myth and cult the society was mirrored. The female component, however, in the form of 'mothers', i.e. protectresses of nature, animals and men, still remained alive in the popular consciousness and formed an important component of their religious world view, the author thinks. Such a development, however, cannot be proved; besides, as Hultkrantz rightly puts forward, 'the existence of female cult figures earlier than the proved existence of male cult figures does not rule out the contemporaneous belief in, say, a male Supreme Being. Inferences from other data – ethnographical, recent sources – suggest this, since such a god is more rarely represented in the art of primitive peoples' (Hultkrantz 1975: 520). Why the wild animals (and the domesticated too) sometimes got a female protectress is because of the 'general character of producer' of Mother Earth in her role of the goddess of birth (Hultkrantz 1961: 85), which is most probable. Furthermore, the Earth Mother was a real Magna Mater figure; she was looked upon as the protectress of the family as a whole – the home, the economy, the members of the family from birth to death – and in all her functions she appeared in different shapes in the view of the peoples; among the Saamis for instance she stayed as Fire Mother, *Sarakka,* who is said to be the 'most beloved one of the divine beings' still in the 18th century.

Summing up we can say that there are common features in the condition of the woman as a social being in the circumpolar hunting and reindeer-herding societies. She is never the dominating member of the group, that is, she does not make the decisions that affect the group as a whole, but among certain peoples she can have a relatively dominant position in the nuclear family, at least in certain matters. She is in other words subordinate, which does not inevitably mean repressed. There are exceptions, however: Castrén, and Donner, observed, as mentioned, that a Siryan woman, and some Samoyed women, for instance lived in a state of socially sanctioned oppression and were treated like irresponsible creatures by men, as the authors interpreted their observations.

Work was strictly divided into male and female tasks, and apparently no one was able to break out of their accustomed roles. The men were the hunters and herders while the women processed their products, took care of the homes and raised the children, the boys in their minority, and were responsible for the chores connected with a nomadic way of life. Here there are also exceptions: among the Selkup a woman could also take part in the hunt (Levin/Potapov 1964: 600); it is said, nonetheless, that she is 'subordinated to the man' but 'her status was not an inferior one'. Hunting and reindeer-keeping are seasonal activities; certain times are filled with hectic work, but these are succeeded by periods of rest. A woman's work does not vary; the entire year is filled with constant labour and therefore she often has a greater burden of work and fewer opportunities to recuperate. A man's life is more flexible, and he therefore comes to be the one who represents the family to the outside world while the woman is less free.

Notes

1 For a Marxist interpretation of matriarchy (with a definition) see Carolyn Fluehr-Lobban 1979.
2 Paine (1972: 79) writes: '. . . a herdsman should be able to handle a reindeer herd in different kinds of terrain, at night as well as by day and in all kinds of weather. This means being able to 'read' the terrain and the weather so that he is able to anticipate the different responses of animals of the various sex and age classes, and be able to deduce the probable whereabouts of sections of the herd that are temporarily missing. Knowledge of winds and different snow conditions are particularly crucial. The able herdsman is also able to recognize the ear-marks, the tones of various reindeer bells, and the natural characteristics of animals in his own and other herds; he is able to remember where and when he saw particular animals or smaller and temporarily unherded flocks.'

3 Transvestism as a socially accepted shamanistic phenomenon has been discussed by Gisela Bleibtreu-Ehrenberg (1970) and others. See also Baumann (1955). This phenomenon can perhaps also be interpreted as follows. Different societies resolve their social problems in different ways. A man, for instance, who is physically weak has difficulties in taking care of himself and a family in a hunting society in an arctic/sub-arctic climate, since the division of labour is made strictly from the point of view of male/female. One way to solve it is for him to assume the role of a woman in his society along with the tasks and behavioural patterns proper to it and, by functioning as a shaman, further legitimize his position (if he has the abilities for that) and be fully accepted as a member of the group. A woman in her turn could abandon her female role and establish herself as a religious guarantor in the group and be accepted as such when she clothed herself in the male role.

4 Heiler (ibid.) describes the engagement of the woman in religion as follows: 'Die Frau steht in ihrem Weibsein in enger Beziehung zu geheimnisvollen, zugleich wertvollen und gefährlichen Mächten; in ihren weiblichen Funktionen (Menstruation, Empfängnis, Geburt) erkennt der primitive Mensch das Wirken der wunderbar-zauberartigen Kraft, des Mana und Tabu, welche die Frau zum religiösen Dienst besonders befähigt. Zu diesen "übernatürlichen" Kräften kommen die besonderen seelischen Eigenschaften der Frau. Ihre starke Sensibilität machen sie zum ekstatisch-visionären Erleben und zur Begeisterungsmantik noch geeigneter als den Mann.'

5 By images here are understood the dolls which a newly married woman in some cases took to her new surroundings from the home of her parents. They represented her personal tutelary spirits (Ränk 1949, 1955, 1966) in a concrete form. They are to be seen as a part of her 'inheritance' from her parents' home.

6 'Uncleanliness' (perhaps 'danger' is preferable), which was associated with a woman in many of the North Eurasian cultures, has attracted the interest of researchers but cannot here be discussed in detail. In a future work we will return to the subject. Here we can only briefly mention that Ränk, for example, sees the 'concept of uncleanliness' from a socio-ethnological angle and believes that the idea of female 'uncleanliness' evolved from the concept of 'alienism', and that this was reinforced by religious restrictions. As has been noted earlier, Ränk holds that this notion only applied to a woman who had married into the group, and as such she was a 'stranger' and thus dangerous. However, according to the available material, a woman entered as a rule into this 'dangerous' position as soon as her first menstruation started, that is, when she assumed an adult role or, according to Saami sources, when she was sexually mature – during the period she was capable of bearing children. Among the Nganasan, a woman was considered 'unclean' only after a pregnancy and childbirth (Levin/Potapov 1964: 577). See Lehtisalo 1924: 113, Karjalainen 1927: 235 f., Rombandjejewa 1963: 85. On the Saami woman see Skanke 1945: 220, Rheen 1897: 39, Reuterskiöld 1910: 36, Leem 1767: 444.

Bibliography

Bachofen, J. K.
1861 Das Mutterrecht: eine Untersuchung über die Gynaikokratie der alten Welt nach ihrer religiosen und rechtlichen Natur. Stuttgart.

Bäckman, L. – Å. Hultkrantz
1978 Studies in Lapp Shamanism. Acta Universitatis Stockholmiensis, Stockholm Studies in Comparative Religion, No. 16. Stockholm.

Baumann, H.
1955 Das doppelte Geschlecht. Ethnologische Studien zur Bisexualität in Ritus und Mythos. Berlin.

Bleibtreu-Ehrenberg, G.
1970 Homosexualität und Transvestition im Schamanismus. Anthropos 65, pp 189–228. Wien.

Castrén, M. A.
1855 Nordiska Resor och Forskningar II. Reseberättelser och Bref åren 1845–1849. Helsingfors.
1870 Nordiska Resor och Forskningar I. Reseminnen från åren 1838—1844. 2nd ed. Helsingfors.

Dieðot.
1979 Boazosámi aemidiid bargodilálašvuoðat. Flyttsamekvinnens arbeidssituasjon No. 4. Karasjokk.

Donner, K.
1915 Bland Samojeder i Sibirien. Åren 1911–1913, 1914. Helsingfors.

Drake, S.
1918 Västerbottenslapparna under förra hälften av 1800-talet. Etnografiska Studier. Lapparna och deras Land. Skildringar och studier utgivna av Hjalmar Lundbohm. VII. Uppsala – Stockholm. New ed. by Två Förläggare Bokförlag. Umeå 1979.

Fluehr-Lobban, C.
1979 A Marxist Reappraisal of the Matriarchate. Current Anthropology, Vol. 20, No. 2, pp 341–348. Comments: pp 608–611. The University of Chicago Press.

Genetz, A.
1891 Wörterbuch der Kola-lappischen Dialekte nebst Sprachproben. Bidrag till kännedom af Finlands natur och folk, 50. Helsingfors.

Graburn, N. H. H. – B. S. Strong
1973 Circumpolar Peoples. An Anthropological Perspective. Pasific Palisades, California.

Grundström, H.
1956 Sarakkagröt – nornegröt – barselgröt – lystenbit. Some Parallels. Arctica. Essays presented to Åke Campbell 1.5 1956. Uppsala.

Harris, M.
1978 Cannibals and Kings: The Origins of Cultures. London.

Harva – see Holmberg (Harva)

Heiler, F.
1977 Die Frau in den Religionen der Menschheit. Berlin.

Högström, P.
(1747) 1980 Beskrifning öfwer de til Sweriges Krona Lydande Lapmarker. (Stockholm.) New ed. by Två Förläggare Bokförlag. Umeå.

Holmberg (Harva), U.
1915 Lappalaisten uskonto. Porvoo. (Also translated into Swedish by P. Bore-

man, revised by K. B. Wiklund. In manuscript at the library of Uppsala university.)

Hultkrantz, Å.
1961 Bachofen and the Mother Goddess. An appraisal after one hundred years. Ethnos 26: 1–2, pp 75–85. Lund.
1975 The Religio-Ecological Method in the Research on Prehistoric Religion. Valcamonica Symposium '72 – Actes sur les Religions de la Préhistoire, Capo di Ponte (ed. Del Centro), pp 519–528.

Itkonen, T. I.
1946 Heidnische Religion und späterer Aberglaube bei den finnischen Lappen. Mémoires de la Société Finno-Ougrienne, 87. Helsinki.

Jettmar, K.
1954 Totemismus und Dualsystem bei den Selkupen Sibiriens. Wiener Völkerkundliche Mitteilungen. Jrg 2, No. 1, pp 21–31. Wien.

Kannisto, A.
1958 Materialen zur Mythologie der Wogulen. Gesammelt von Artturi Kannisto, bearbeitet und herausgegeben von E. A. Virtanen und Matti Liimola. Mémoires de la Société Finno-Ougrienne, 113. Helsinki.

Karjalainen, K. F.
1927 Die Religion der Jugra-Völker III. Folklore Fellows Communications, 20. Helsinki – Porvoo.

Kildal, J.
1945 Afguderiets Dempelse. Nordnorske Samlinger. Vol. V. Oslo.

Kjellström, R.
1969 Lapparnas frierier och bröllop. Fataburen, pp 193–218. Stockholm.
1973 Eskimo Marriage. An Account of Traditional Eskimo Courtship and Marriage. Nordiska museets Handlingar 80. Lund.

König, H.
1929 Das Recht der Polarvölker. Anthropos 24, pp 621–664. Wien.

Kristoffer Sjulssons minnen om Vapstenlapparna i början af 1800-talet. Upptecknade af O. P. Pettersson, ed. by L. Bäckman–R. Kjellström. Acta Lapponica 20. Nordiska museet 1979. Lund.

Leem, K.
1767 Beskrivelse over Finmarkens Lapper, deres Tungemaal, Levemaade og forrige Afgudsdyrkelse, oplyst ved mange Kobberstykker. Kiøbenhavn.

Lehtisalo, T.
1924 Entwurf einer Mythologie der Jurak-Samojeden. Mémoires de la Société Finno-Ougrienne, 63. Helsinki.

Levin, M. G. – L. P. Potapov, eds.
1964 The Peoples of Siberia. Chicago and London.

Lid, N.
1946 Light-Mother and Earth-Mother. Studia Norvegica, No. 4, pp 3–20. Oslo.

Maringer, J.
1977 Priests and Priestesses in Prehistoric Europe. History of Religions, Vol. 17, No. 1, pp 101–120. Chicago.
1979 Die Frau in den vorgeschichtlichen Religionen. Anthropos, 74, Wien.

Nahodil, O.
1963 Mutterkult in Sibirien. Glaubenswelt und Folklore der sibirischen Völker, ed. by V. Diószegi, pp 491–511. Budapest.

Neumann, E.
1956 Die grosse Mutter. Der Archetyp des grossen Weiblichen. Zürich.

Paine, R.
1972 The Herd Management of Lapp Reindeer Pastoralists. Perspectives on

Nomadism. International Studies in Sociology and Social Anthropology, ed. by W. Irons – N. Dyson-Hudson. Leiden.

Prokofyeva, Y. D.
1963 The Costume of an Enets Shaman. Studies in Siberian Shamanism, ed. by H. N. Michael, pp 124–156. Arctic Institute of North America. Anthropology of the North: Translations from Russian Sources No. 4. Toronto.

Ränk, G.
1948 Die Hausgottheiten der Frauen und das Geschlechtstabu bei den nordeurasischen Völkern. Ethnos 13: 3–4, pp 153–170. Lund.
1955 Lapp Female Deities of the Madder-akka group. Studia Septentrionalia, Vol. VI. Oslo.
1966 Mannen, kvinnan och släkten hos nordeurasiska jägare och fiskare. Kulturspeglingar. Stockholm.

Reuterskiöld, E., ed.
1910 Källskrifter till lapparnas mytologi. Bidrag till vår odlings häfder, No. 10. Stockholm.

Rheen, S.
1897 En kortt Relation om Lapparnes Lefwarne och Sedher, wijd-Skiepellsser sampt i många Stycken Grofwe wildfarellsser. Svenska Landsmål XVII: 1. Uppsala.

Rombandjejewa, E. I.
1963 Einige Sitten und Bräuche der Mansen (Wogulen) bei der Geburt der Kinder. Glaubenswelt und Folklore der sibirischen Völker, ed. by V. Diószegi, pp 85–92. Budapest.

Rytcheu, J.
1980 Tjuktjerfolkets historia kan liknas med samernas. Tidningen Samefolket, No. 1. Östersund.

Shimkin, D. B.
1939 A Sketch of the Ket, or Yenisei 'Ostyak'. Ethnos, 4: 3–4, pp 147–176. Lund.

Simčenko, J. B.
1978 Mother Cult among the North-Eurasian Peoples. Shamanism in Siberia, ed. by V. Diószegi – M. Hoppál, pp 503–513. Budapest.

Skanke, H.
1945 Epitomes Historiae Missionis Lapponicae. 1: De Nordske Lappers Hedendom og Superstitioner. Nordnorske Samlinger, Vol. V. Oslo.

Solem, E.
1933 Lappiske rettsstudier. Oslo.

Vilkuna, A.
1956 Das Verhalten der Finnen in heiligen (pyhä) Situationen. Folklore Fellows Communications, 164. Helsinki.

Religion and Experience of Nature among North American Hunting Indians

Åke Hultkrantz

I

About the turn of the eighteenth century the French traveller Baron de Lahontan made interesting observations among the Algonkian-speaking Indians of northeastern North America. Whenever an event took place in nature, he says, when a branch of a tree hurt a person's eye, or a ferocious storm upset a lake, these Indians first of all asked themselves who could have caused this event, what spirit was responsible (de Lahontan 1905 II: 446). Thus, there was here a direct association between religion and occurrences in nature. American Indian religion made the impression of being a cult of nature, 'naturism'.

Such ideas of the origins of religion slowly paved their way after the great geographic discoveries when the knowledge spread of cultures and religions closer to nature than those known before, in the Mediterranean area and the Middle East. While man's identification with nature plays a major role in some thinkers of Romanticism – the nature pantheism of Friedrich Creuzer, the nature mythology of Adalbert Kuhn, Wilhelm Schwartz and Max Müller – it was within the frame of evolutionistic thought that religious origins were referred to man's experience of nature. For example, John Lubbock outlines the 'first great stages in religious thought', beginning with atheism, fetishism and 'nature-worship, or totemism, in which natural objects, trees, lakes, stones, animals, etc. are worshipped' (Lubbock 1870: 119). Edward Burnett Tylor followed suit, although he saw the basic origins of religion in 'the doctrine of souls'.

In the evolutionistic perspective of these anthropologists 'primitive man' was throughout dominated by the play of the natural forces. German scholars invented the cliché 'nature peoples' (*Naturvölker*) in distinction to 'culture peoples' (*Kulturvölker*), a distinction that provoked Karl Weule to refer to primitive man's cultural heritage as 'the culture of peoples without culture' (*die Kultur der Kulturlosen*) (Weule 1921). The implication was of course that 'nature peoples' were ethnic groups that in their cultural life were critically dependent on their natural environment. Such groups were hunters, collectors and fishermen. It was among them that the dependence upon the natural forces was transformed into a belief in spirits and gods ruling over nature and over man as well.

It is interesting to study how the evolutionists imagined the process of this transformation. Tylor quotes an observer at the end of the eighteenth century, Römer, who visited a fetish house in Guinea. He peeped in and found an old man sitting there amid thousands of fetishes, collected by him and his ancestors. 'The visitor took up a stone about as big as a hen's egg, and its owner told its history. He was once going out on important business, but crossing the threshold he trod on this stone and hurt himself. Ha ha! thought he, art thou here? So he took the stone, and it helped him through his undertaking for days' (Tylor 1891 II: 158). Tylor presumed of course that it was the spirit in the fetish that made it work. Nevertheless, the adoption of new fetishes is presented in a somewhat mechanical way.

A similar although more refined standpoint was taken by R. R. Marett. He writes, 'What we call "physical nature" may very well be "nature" also to the savage in most of its normal aspects: yet its more startling manifestations, thunderstorms, eclipses, eruptions, and the like, are eminently calculated to awake in him an Awe that I believe to be specifically religious both in its essence and in its fruits' (Marett 1909: 14; cf. 19). As late as 1935 another scholar, Rafael Karsten, suggested that the belief in such natural phenomena as supernatural 'must ultimately be explained by the savage people's ignorance of what we call natural laws' (Karsten 1935: 133).

So far the evolutionists of the old school. We know today that man's patterns of perception and values are the results of a long cultural tradition. Consequently, spirits and gods are formed after premises residing in the different cultural systems. If an African bestows the status of fetish on a stone, he does so in accordance with the ruling patterns of his culture. The faith is there, the beliefs are there, and the expectations of supranormal courses of events are there as well. It is easy to agree with Harold Turner when he says:

Although it is patent that environment conditions, and promotes or inhibits, the different possible patterns and forms of religions around the world, one must reject

the mid-19th century theories that religion is due to man's reaction to certain phenomena in nature which arouse fear, wonder or puzzlement; and that religions are
therefore man's rather mistaken attempts to come to terms with an environment that
otherwise he can neither control nor understand (Turner 1976: 12).

The fact remains, however, that hunting peoples' religions disclose a
stronger connection with natural phenomena than other religions. The
problem arises as to what role we should ascribe to man's experience of
nature in the formation of hunting religions. With reference to what has
already been said we may safely presume that man's impressions of nature actually bring to the fore and strengthen tendencies that are part of
the pattern of religious traditions. It would seem more doubtful that an
experience of nature could create new religious conceptions, new in relation to the prevalent pattern. Or is such an occurrence possible?

In order to illuminate this problem I shall now turn to an analysis of
the pattern of North American hunting religions, typified in the religion
of the Ojibway Indians.[1]

II

Aboriginal North America included a series of hunting cultures of a
changing profile from the technologically specialized foraging culture of
the Eskimo, concentrated upon seal hunting, to the impoverished culture
of the Gosiute Indians in Utah, characterized by the hunting of small
animals and collecting economy. Also from a sociological point of view
the gap may sometimes be considerable between different sorts of hunting
cultures: for instance, we have the stratified societies of the North Pacific
Coast but also the more democratic social structures among the hunting
Indians of the Eastern Woodlands and Plains. Thus, every effort to portray *the* North American hunting culture goes wrong and remains a fic-
tion. Still, there are many things common to all hunting cultures in North
America. To some extent they are also common to hunting cultures in
northern Eurasia, but it seems that some elements belong exclusively to
North America.

In two respects the North American hunting cultures had a stronger
hold than their Eurasian counterparts. First of all, they were basic everywhere. A study of, for instance, Clark Wissler's map of culture area
distributions makes it evident that plant cultivators lived in restricted
areas: in the Southwest (in particular the Pueblo Indians of New Mexico
and Arizona), along the lower reaches of the Missouri (Siouan and Cad-

doan tribes), and in the Eastern Woodlands (Iroquois, some Algonkian and Siouan groups, Muskhogi and others), with concentration to the south (Wissler 1950: 2, 221, cf. Driver 1961: maps 3–4). Hunting peoples are thus to be found in the whole of northern and western North America, in particular in the culture areas now passing under the denominations Arctic and Subarctic cultures, on the Northwest Coast and the Plateau, in the Great Basin, California and Plains Indian culture area,[2] and on the Gulf Coast. It is true that Northwest Coast Indians were predominantly fishermen and the Basin and California Indians predominantly collectors, but hunting nevertheless played a major role in their existence. Indeed, hunting was also an important occupation among the maize cultivators. As a matter of fact, as we can find out from modern surveys, hunting was often more valuable economically than agriculture in the northern parts of the Eastern Woodlands (cf. Trigger 1978). There were no North American cultures without hunting traditions.

Secondly, as has been pointed out particularly by John Witthoft, the basic cultural structure in the Eastern Woodlands was that of the hunter (Witthoft 1949: 84; cf. Hultkrantz 1979 d: 144 ff.). This means that the ideas and the behaviour patterns pertaining to maize cultivation had directly been stimulated by the idea system of the hunting culture. In other words, the religious ideology of the hunting culture permeated most North American cultures. We could possibly make an exception for the fertility ideology of the Pueblo Indians and the sacred system of the Southeastern Indians; they had ultimately been inspired from Mexican high cultures.

This strong position of the hunting cultures created the necessary conditions for a diffusion over wide areas of hunting conceptions and hunting rites (provided their occurrence was not due to a common archaic heritage). Predominant among these beliefs and customs were those that were attached to the game and its killing. In principle we are here facing the same complex of phenomena that we recognize among Arctic and Subarctic peoples in Siberia, known as 'Jagdriten' (Holmberg) or 'rites de chasse' (Lot-Falck).

In North America this complex includes various beliefs about the animals. Here belong notions about the animals as the equals of man,[3] about their distribution into tribes, and their possession of souls of the same kind, or a similar kind, as those of man (Hultkrantz 1953: 483 ff.). The bear is granted a particular position, since it is considered to have an intelligence comparable with man's and moreover can walk around like man on its hind legs. It is therefore natural that the bear has the same set of souls as man. All animals are treated with respect and even reverence, and they are buried in their natural surroundings (on the ground or in the water). Particular care is taken that the bones of the skeleton are arranged in an anatomical order, although the skull is often disposed of separately (cf. Paulson 1959: 182 ff.). The whole complex of beliefs and observances is known as animal ceremonialism. It has reached its peak in the so-called bear cult, an historically connected assemblage of beliefs and rituals extending from the Saamis (Lapps) in the west to the Lenape (Delaware) on the Atlantic Coast in the east (Hallowell 1926). In North America the bear cult has reached as far south as the Southwestern Indians (Paproth 1976: 18 ff.). Characteristic of the bear cult in both continents are, inter alia, the hunter's apology to the animal he has killed, the sacred meal on the bear, and the removal of his skull to a tree (Paulson 1965: 150 ff.).

Hunting magic of various kinds promotes hunting luck. The hunter covers himself with talismans like pebbles, claws, fetish bags with feathers, skins or other selected objects. (Such 'medicine bags' were mostly granted the individual by personal guardian spirits that revealed their composition in dreams and visions, see e.g. Speck and Heye 1921.) The medicine-man sinks into ecstasy in order to disclose the hidden whereabouts of the game. In dreams even common Indians may see the animal that will be his prey. Another divinatory technique is the scapulimancy, diffused in the far north (Hultkrantz 1968: 69 ff.). The hunter watched favourable forebodings, for instance, an unexpected meeting with a lucky animal, or he took caution from an unfavourable foreboding, for instance a woman crossing the trail. Hunting luck is safeguarded through ritual dances in which the hunter imitates the animals and kills them symbolically.

It is common that the animals are protected and ruled by a supernatural master, one for each species, or one for the animals, another for the fishes, or even one for the whole animal world. This master or owner allows the hunter to kill the animals or holds them back so he cannot find them. In the latter case it is usually supposed that a taboo has been transgressed by the hunter or his family. The master may be described as the prototype of the animal species, its 'soul' (Hultkrantz 1961: 53 ff., Paulson 1964: 202 ff.).

In tribal myths representatives of the animals occupy a prominent place. It is significant that the culture hero, the mythic originator of many rituals and profane institutions, is visualized in theriomorphic shape. The Great Hare, Coyote, and Raven are some of the most well-known culture heroes. According to some scholars, the culture hero was from the outset a master of the animals (Pettazzoni 1954: 21 ff., Kock 1956: 126 ff.).

All these beliefs and practices associated with the animals are not evenly represented among the North American hunting tribes but show different areas of diffusion. Thus, animal ceremonialism belongs primarily to the Arctic and Subarctic areas and the Plains. The bear cult has its focus in the north. The scapulimancy has a Canadian-Siberian-Chinese dissemination. The concept of the master of the animals is most prolific among the northern Algonkians but also exists elsewhere. On the Plains and the Plateau and in the Great Basin this concept has been ousted by the idea of individual guardian spirits intensely developed here: the guardian spirit of the hunter alone warrants the hunting luck. In the Southwest, on the other hand, the masters of the animals appear again.

In the same way as the guardian spirits, other spiritual beings not primarily associated with hunting may also become connected with the hunting complex. Thus, the Supreme Being sometimes displays the functions of a master of the animals, for example, among the Cree (Cooper 1933: 53, 61 and passim). The Winds, the Thunder, and supernatural maidens may among other things also appear as the protectors of the animals (e.g. Feit 1973: 54 ff.: the North Wind, Chuetenshu, among the Cree; Dorsey 1905: 46 ff.: the Thunder; Brown 1953: 3 ff.: the Buffalo maiden). The great tribal ceremony sometimes includes as an essential part the idea of a recreation of the animals, as the Sun Dance of the Cheyenne clearly demonstrates (Dorsey 1905: 46, cf. Hultkrantz 1980 a: 241). In all prayers directed to the powers we find the hopes that the animals might thrive and the hunting luck be good.

For obvious reasons the world of the hunter is primarily focused on the wild game. However, he also has an eye for the wider environment to which both he himself and the animals belong. He observes and knows the forest, the plains, the mountains, and the waters. They are part of his world picture and have their particular spirits to whom he has to pay respect and, as occasion requires, make sacrifices (usually tobacco offerings). In this connection we can make an important observation: the wild nature is as a rule no frightening world to the Indian hunter (for exceptions, see below). He knows, for instance, the forest and all its secrets. He was born and grew up there; it is his home and the familiar world where he seeks the animals. In this respect he differs considerably from the thoroughbred agriculturist, who tends to regard his immediate surroundings and the outer environment – the cultivated country and the undeveloped country – as contrasting realities. 'Wilderness' is a part of the world of the agriculturist, but it has no place in the conceptual world of the hunter (cf. Müller 1972: 29, quoting Standing Bear, Teton chief).

The situation in aboriginal times in northern Eurasia offers a good illustration of this dualism. Ivar Paulson has stressed that in this large area the forest has become, in the conceptual world of the peasants, an outside world ('Aussenkreis') with many dangers and hasards (Paulson 1961: 278). Agriculture and cattle-breeding 'haben den Menschen vom Wild und der Wildnis, bzw. vom Wasser und den Fischen entwöhnt. Die sog. Aussenkreise (die wilde Natur der Wälder und des Wassers) erscheinen dem an seinen Hof und Acker gebundenen Bauer als unheimliche, unheilsvolle Bereiche, wo böse Mächte und schreckliche Wesen herrschen' (Paulson 1961: 280). It is true that the polarization of the world picture is less apparent among North American Indians, who are often hunter and agriculturist in the same person. Still, we perceive the same general orientation towards two different concepts of the environment among hunters and peasants in American aboriginal cultures.[4]

The foregoing general statements on American Indian hunting religions will now be tested and exemplified with the information we have of a rather pronounced hunting religion, that of the Ojibway Indians. This religion should have a particular interest for us, since the Ojibway outlook on their environment in important aspects was recently analyzed by Calvin Martin (1978) and Christopher Vecsey (1980). It will be our particular task to investigate whether natural environment plays the formative role for religious conceptions that was intimated in the foregoing, or whether it simply served as a background for religious ideas or, on the contrary, by force of its dramatic and overpowering character created particular prerequisites for religious developments.

III

From their earliest known hunting grounds north of Sault Ste. Marie the Ojibway Indians (also called Chippewa in the United States, Saulteaux in Canada) have extended their territory during the course of the seventeenth and eighteenth centuries. They dispersed partly south and southwest of the Great Lakes, partly towards the north-west, to the areas around the Lake Winnipeg and west of this lake (see the ethnohistorical reconstructions in Hickerson 1962 b, 1967 and 1970). This expansion was accompanied by great cultural changes. The static picture of the

Ojibway society still prominent among scholars in the 1930s suggested that these Indians were hunters with a bilateral social structure, and that each family had their allotted territory or 'family hunting grounds' (cf. Speck 1915, Cooper 1939). However, the clear traces of totemism found among some Ojibway were difficult to combine with this picture. Ethno-historical investigations during the past thirty years have shown that the individualized family organization with separate hunting grounds primarily belongs to the north-western Ojibway, and that the latter are relative late-comers, trappers who have exploited hunting grounds which earlier belonged to the Cree and other Algonkian groups (Bishop 1976). The incentive of this development was the European-American fur trade.[5]

We find here a situation that almost everywhere in North America jeopardizes the efforts of scholars to reach ethnological and religio-historical syntheses: the data at our disposal are contained in an historical course of events and consequently represent a particular phase of an historical development. The Ojibway have certainly always been hunters and fishermen, but not only that, and their social structure and other economic occupations have changed considerably during the three hundred years they have been known to us. It deserves mentioning that almost all the great changes we know of were directly or indirectly caused by the political, cultural and religious aspirations of the whites.

It is possible to discern the following main periods in Ojibway culture history: (1) A protohistorical period when the people lived on hunting and fishing and gathered in villages. These settlements constituted the basis for unilinear – probably patrilinear – totemistic clans.[6] (2) A period of transition characterized by an intense commercial exchange with other Indians and white traders in Sault Ste. Marie during the summer months (the middle of the seventeenth century). (3) As a result of the fur trade a migration to new areas and a dissolution of the old clan society. In Michigan and southern Ontario the Ojibway took up cultivation of maize and squash; north of the Great Lakes they tapped maple sugar, and partly engaged themselves in wild rice harvesting; in Wisconsin and Minnesota the latter occupation was most important; farther west they turned into horsemen who hunted bison on the Plains during the course of the eighteenth century.

It would naturally have been advantageous if we had possessed source materials illuminating the religion during the oldest period mentioned here. (Or even, for that matter, if we had sources from the remote times when as 'palaeo-Indians' the ancestors of the Ojibway hunted the Late Pleistocene macrofauna, mammoths, giant bisons, and other now extinct

170

animals.) The well-known anthropologist Irving Hallowell maintained that those latter-day Ojibway who had made their homes in the woody and swampy grounds east of Lake Winnipeg preserved through their isolated situation many older cultural elements which, in his opinion, have descended from the 'original' Ojibway (Hallowell 1955: 112, 233 f.). We could also express the matter thus: that the maintenance of one and the same culture-ecological structure facilitated the cultural continuity. An examination of the religious life of these groups gives us information on a religious pattern that has retained much of its character through the centuries. John Cooper and Irving Hallowell have provided us with the best documents we have on recent Ojibway religion (Cooper 1936, Hallowell 1934, 1942, 1960). The most detailed information on the integration of religion with nature has been delivered by Diamond Jenness in his treatise on the Parry Island Ojibway (Jenness 1935). Further materials on the man-animal relationships among the closely related Cree-Mistassini may be found in a recent book by Adrian Tanner (1979). A forthcoming work by Christopher Vecsey will summarize the wealth of information on the Ojibway Indians (Vecsey Ms.).

As should have emerged from the foregoing, the Ojibway Indians, the protohistorical as well as the latter-day woodland Indians in western Ontario, were hunters, fishermen and collectors. Theirs was a strenuous life (cf. Kohl 1859 I: 285, 290). As hunters they brought down moose, woodland caribou, deer, bears, beavers, and other game of the forest. Presumably there was more game in the protohistorical homelands around Lake Superior and Lake Huron than in the marked woodland areas of western Ontario, even before the great depletion of the game brought about by the organized fur trade (cf. Bishop 1976: 49). The dwellings were dome-shaped wigwams, covered by birch-bark; household utensils and canoes were also made from bark or wood. In protohistorical times the Indians lived together in big villages (appropriate settlements for fishing and trade), except during the winter, when they hunted in small groups. Village life probably stimulated religious gatherings of a kind that only in faded forms exist among latter-day Ojibway in Ontario.[7]

It is difficult to give an account of Ojibway Indian religion, since religious ideas differ from one locality to another and individual respondents have often been unable to state what they really believed in. Interpretations therefore vary considerably (cf. Jenness 1935: 32). Here follows however an attempt at categorizing the religion of the woodland Ojibway.

(1) World picture: The earth rests as a disk between the sky world (sometimes thought to have six floors) and the world below (which was also sometimes envisaged to have six levels). It is kept in place by the Milky Way, the latter also identified as the road of souls to the land of the dead (Jenness 1935: 28). Since the Milky Way also functions as the cosmic pillar of the world, it may furthermore be imagined as a vine or a ladder used by the spirits when from on high they descend to earth (Copway 1850: 170). The four corners of the world are ruled by four spirits, of which the one in the north is the master of the winds. Up in heaven the Supreme Being rules over the whole scene: the Great Spirit (Manitou, Kitchi Manitou). In the world of myths there is also the culture hero Nanibush, the Great Hare. The southern Ojibway know also the evil spirit, Matchi Manitou, probably a late-comer in the pantheon.

(2) Main cosmic powers: The Great Spirit is 'boss of the whole thing,' he gives food to man when supplicated to do so, and he is sometimes represented as a master of the animals. It is uncertain whether the sun and the moon were regarded as divine beings who received a cult (the southern Ojibway seem to have made offerings to them). The thunder was now conceived of as an anthropomorphic thunderer – perhaps identical with the Supreme Being – now conceived of as a number of thunderers; or it was represented as one or several thunderbirds. During thunderstorms tobacco was offered in the fire to these beings. Stone constructions on elevated places may have been envisaged as the nests of the thunderbirds (Hallowell 1960: 156). The rumbling of the thunder is interpreted as an oral message by some Ojibway. Severe thunderstorms are understood as wars between the thunderers and the big (mythical) water-snakes that are the enemies of man as well. The winds are closely associated with the thunderers. In stormy weather tobacco is thrown into the water for them. There is, finally, 'grandmother Earth' who receives offerings when trees or roots are cut down or removed.

(3) The cult directed to the animals: Both the Supreme Being and the masters of the different species of animals are supposed to look after the game. The belief in animal masters seems to have been more systematized among the southern Ojibway than among their northern kinsmen; among the latter the high god appears to have functioned as the owner of the animals quite frequently (cf. e.g. Cooper 1936: 22 f.). The masters of the animals resemble the animals but are bigger and always have a white colour. They sometimes show themselves to the Indians who then are allowed to kill them (Jenness 1935: 23). (Also trees and plants have su-

pernatural masters, distinguished by their height, and they may similarly be brought down.)

The care that the master of the animals gives his clients may also be tendered by the animals themselves: since the animals have psychic qualities they can of their own accord keep away from the hunter if the latter has defiled one of their kind. They communicate between themselves and widely convey the message of the taboo infliction to all the other animals and, of course, also to their master. On the other hand, the animals are propitiated by the rites earlier discussed as 'animal ceremonialism'. Thus, the Ojibway promise the bear that they are going to serve him exquisite food, and when the bear has been killed both the hunters and the bear feast on the food – the hunters realistically, the bear symbolically (Cooper 1936: 23). The skull of the bear is placed in a tree and his bones laid down out of reach of the dogs and wild animals. The bear soul is supposed to travel to the lower world to be reborn later, according to some informants, with exactly the same bones it had had in this life (Jenness 1935: 25). Other animals too were treated with deference, although not as circumstantially as the bear. For instance, the bones of the beaver had to be treated carefully; dogs were not allowed to touch them, and the patella had to be lowered into the water. Birds' wings were hung up in trees.

The close connection between man and animals made the Ojibway very conscious of the presence of the animals. George Copway's parents forbade their little boy to be noisy and sing in the forest, for the forest belongs to the animals, and the animals do not want to be disturbed by the clamour of people (Müller 1976: 45, quoting Copway 1851: 18).

(4) Magic conceptions and customs surrounding the hunting: They are legion. As an example will be presented here the following practices to secure hunting luck among the Ojibway of the Lake of the Woods area. Before the hunt Indians try to influence their luck through singing and drumming. If it is winter, they swing a bull-roarer to achieve the formation of a crust on the snow. When caribou are to be hunted the hunter wears a bezoar from the caribou as a talisman, and when rabbits are to be hunted he ties the foetal inclusion of a rabbit to the snare. Through various kinds of divination the hunting party tries to find out the whereabouts of the game. Among these devices are scapulimancy, or divination from cracks in animal bones (for instance, shoulder blades) that have been heated over fire; the shaking tent rite, in which the medicine-man calls on his helping spirits to give information (their entrance makes the tent shake); crystal gazing (in water or a mirror); and

interpretation from the movements of a bear's patella over hot sands or a fire (Cooper 1936: 7 ff.).

(5) The guardian spirit complex: Nature abounds with spirits. 'The earth teemed with all sorts of spirits, good and bad; those of the forest clothed themselves with moss. During a shower of rain, thousands of them are sheltered in a flower' (Copway 1850: 153). The majority of the spirits appear in theriomorphic shapes, but also other forms occur. There are the 'wild people' or dwarfs, harmless goblins who may be heard in the spring, and 'memegwesio', hairless small beings that roam about in rocky places and may help man to find the game; they also seem to rule over the wind. There are also solitary spirits like Pagak, the skeleton being whom one can hear whistling up in the air, another harmless supernatural, and Windigo or Witiko, a monstrous giant living on human meat, probably a symbolical prototype of those human beings who during the starvation periods of the winter are compelled to cannibalism (cf. Parker 1960, Teicher 1960). With few exceptions all these spirits, but in particular the zoomorphic spirits, may function as a man's guardian spirits, and that on two levels:

(a) Individual guardian spirits. Youths in their early puberty, or even before, try to acquire a guardian spirit that will henceforth protect them through the changes of life. Alone or in groups they seek out a place that is isolated and lonely, a hill, a rock out in a lake, sometimes a tree-top, where they build a platform looking like a bird's nest. Here they wait for the arrival of the spirit, perhaps for several days, all the time fasting. Finally the guardian spirit turns up in a dream or vision (see Radin 1936).

(b) Totem spirits. An examination of the totemic spirits, that is, the spirits whose names are attached to the different clans and who are supposed vaguely to protect them shows, that in many cases they have been identical with the guardian spirits of the individual (Hultkrantz 1972: 223 f., Flannery 1940: 23). Perhaps this situation was the cause that totemism and individual guardian-spirit beliefs were confounded in Long's definition of totemism (Long 1791: 86 f., cf. comments in Dunning 1959: 79 f. and Hultkrantz 1979 d: 66 f.). It was, by the way, these northern Ojibway that Long had in mind when he coined the term 'totemism'. However, as a matter of fact totemism is weaker among the northern and western Ojibway than among the southern Ojibway – another factor that may have contributed to Long's mistake (Dunning 1959: 82). Among several Ojibway today the totem is just a name of

174

the clan (Landes 1937: 31). Among other Ojibway totemism is more substantial, and parts of the totem animal are taboo to eat (Skinner 1911: 150).

(6) The medicine-men: They are, as in other parts of North America, religio-magical specialists who stand apart from other recipients of supernatural power in the sense that their power is greater and directed to curing and (or) divination. Ojibway medicine-man are, also in the north, divided into several classes, 'surgeons', herbal doctors, midewiwin shamans, seers, shaking tent diviners, and fire-eaters. Of these the 'surgeons' have received their secret powers by fasting longer than other participants in the vision quest. Their curing method is to suck out the evil that has caused a disease, usually an object or a spirit, through a bone tube made from the wing of a goose. It is uncertain whether the other great curing method, the trance journey of the medicine-man to catch a lost or runaway soul, has occurred among the northern Ojibway. As said before, the midewiwin is a society of medicine-men arisen through influences from the south. It contains one original Ojibway feature, the cosmic perspective that among other hunting peoples belongs to the new year's rites.

(7) Conceptions of the dead: The dead person is supposed to cross a rapid on a slippery stock before he reaches the land of the dead – a migratory motif that had a wide dissemination in North America (Hultkrantz 1980 b: 173). The exact location of the land of the dead is uncertain. All or almost all the dead seem to come there, but those who have transgressed social law are referred to marginal parts of this realm (Cooper 1936: 21).

The dead may appear as guardian spirits, and at meals meat is offered for them in the fire (cf. Hultkrantz 1978: 110 f.). Otherwise we do not find many reminiscences of the feast of the dead that was celebrated among the southern Ojibway and that was a heritage from more southerly cultural horizons (see above).

This ends our survey of Ojibway religion. The close integration between this religion and nature is evident, and it is apparent even today. When in 1962 the Ojibway of Grassy Narrows, Ontario, were forced to move to a new place they were struck by diseases from mercury poisoning. Some older men commented, 'Maybe the spirits here aren't good. Anyway, they were never consulted' (Erikson and Vecsey 1980: 157). Old John Beaver found that since there were no curers, no shaking tents, and no vision quests the reserve was of course destructive for the people (Vecsey Ms).

IV

Our investigation of the Ojibway hunting religion leads us to the following conclusions.

It is obvious that the Ojibway religion – in any case among the Canadian woodland Ojibway – reflected the natural environment in a powerful way. This is scarcely surprising, since these Indians were to a great extent susceptible to the play of natural forces. Outside of the social community their closest environment was nature itself, and they lived on what nature could give them. There are in particular two points that should be stressed here: (1) the natural environment stands out as an obvious frame of reference for religious symbolism; (2) the necessary economical exploitation of the animal world is a source of religious activation and a pressing cause of religious speculation.

On the other hand, many religious phenomena, in particular the world view and the eschatology, lack an obvious reference to natural environment, or are only secondarily connected with it. Thus, the Supreme Being may act as an animal master, but his primary task is certainly to shield the world and assist mankind independently of the quality of the environment. Other religious phenomena, for instance, certain eschatological notions have a diffusion that transcends the Ojibway area. It would therefore be misleading to say that all aspects of Ojibway religion disclose natural influences.

How should we then characterize the impact of natural environment on Ojibway religion? In order to understand this relationship we have to apply the teachings of the religio-ecological model as elaborated by myself in earlier papers (cf. in particular Hultkrantz 1979 a). This model shows that there is an environmental influence on religion that stands in relation to the cultural dependence on nature. Julian Steward has demonstrated that there is an ecological integration between nature and culture in which nature not only inhibits but also promotes cultural development (Steward 1955). This argument has certain repercussions on religious developments as well (although Steward did not observe it). At least in principle, for historical circumstances, as well as the conservative tendencies of religion, complicate the picture. The religio-ecological integration can most clearly be observed in the cultures that are the most primitive in material and technological respects. To a certain extent Ojibway culture belongs here.

Briefly put, there are several levels of religio-ecological integration, which I have called primary, secondary, and morphological integration. The first one includes environmental adaptation of basic cultural features like subsistence and technology and the religous features associated with them, for instance, animal ceremonialism (which is indeed a 'subsistence ritual'). In the secondary integration there is an indirect adaptation of religious beliefs and practices: the latter are organized in forms that derive from the social structure, which is, in its turn, more or less dependent on a primary ecological integration. The egalitarian and slightly chaotic character of the Ojibway spiritual world may be taken as an example. The morphological integration, again, is more direct: religious features take their forms from the physical and biological environment. The zoomorphic apparitions of the visionary spirits and the masters of the animals among the Ojibway come easily to mind.

It is important to realize that the ecological impact through primary or secondary integration refers to the general patterns of religious ideas and rites, not to their exact contents, which are dependent on historical factors and man's personal inspiration. One could say that the design of religious ideas is an ecological process, whereas their contents – whether expressions of faith, confidence or fright in relation to a supernatural power – have a deeper, religious motivation.

From this angle natural environment constitutes a frame of reference which may stimulate the growth of religious forms, but not basically call new religious feelings into being. Religion depends upon nature, but its source is man. Here, however, we may ask whether the Ojibway concept of the Windigo does not prove that religious ideas may be derived from radical experiences of nature that have broken through the conventional pattern of religious cognition. Scholars have claimed that this is a matter of deep-going experiences of hunger, a human attitude to the surrounding environment provoked in a situation of destitution and physiological weakness. It has been suggested that the hunger experiences have followed in the footsteps of devastating diseases: among the northern Athapascan tribes in Canada periods of severe starvation coincide with periods of extreme ill health (Krech 1978: 717). Whatever our reactions to this suggestion – it could just as well be the other way round – hunger and starvation have always been well-known phenomena among the Indians of interior Canada. However, there are two reasons why we should not consider Windigo an invention of starving Ojibway and Cree Indians. Firstly, we find similar cannibal beings in the folklore and religion of Indian tribes living in warmer climates (cf. Thompson 1929: 351). Secondly, the northern Athapascans who live in just as hard and merciless a climate as the Ojibway, and who often have starved during the winter, do not know any supernatural cannibal spirit. It is therefore probable that the Ojibway have inherited the conception of the Windigo from very remote times.

For the rest, empirical evidence tells us that Indians when surprised by the violent, eruptive forces of nature do not change but modestly adapt their religious picture after the new experiences. In another place I have tried to describe how Indian reactions varied to the spouting geysers of the Yellowstone Park area: for Indians living at a distance this area was dangerous and tabooed, whereas the Shoshonean Sheepeaters who lived there neutralized the dangers by imagining the geysers to be occupied by spiritual beings formed after the old Shoshonean mould and by adjusting their traditional ritual system to these spirits (Hultkrantz 1954, cf. Hultkrantz 1979 c). In other words, natural miracles do not change the religious pattern, but are incorporated into the latter. A similar case of incorporation seems actually to have occurred among the Parry Island Ojibway, for they believe that earthquakes are caused by a thunder being (Jenness 1935: 37).

The impact of nature on religion is easier to discover in the strength that certain conceptions have in comparison with others. Shamanism for instance has been elaborated among the Ojibway to a high extent. We have seen how highly classified the medicine-men were in Ojibway society, how they were involved as diviners of the game and as doctors. The latter role deserves our further attention. Diseases were frequent and had an effect on the population trend that has only in our days been fully appreciated by ethnologists (cf. Dobyns 1976). In early aboriginal times the severity of the winter climate and the periodical malnutrition certainly undermined public health. In post-contact times the ravages of epidemic diseases no doubt furthered the importance of the inspired healer.[8]

The watchful reader should have noticed that no regard has been given to the argument, discussed by psychologists of religion in the past, that moving, esthetic experiences of nature stimulate the growth of religion. It has sometimes been claimed that Indians in their meditation experienced both feelings of loftiness and rapture and feelings of harmony and order when facing the beauty of nature. This is correct; but it was not nature as such that inspired these feelings, it was – as I have tried to show in other connections – the very fact that nature revealed God or the supernatural world that made nature beautiful, sacred (Hultkrantz

1979 b, 1981: 117 ff.). In Ojibway religion there is nothing that lends support to the expectation that meditation upon nature engendered religious beliefs.

We shall now see why this had to be so.

V

On numerous occasions in the past I have been able to observe that North American Indians easily adopt a symbolic outlook on religion. By symbol I here mean any result of an effort to describe a human experience that challenges adequate description (cf. Hultkrantz Ms). The Sioux Indian, Ohiyesa, born and brought up among his tribesmen on the Plains but later educated as a medical doctor in white society, has said the following wise words concerning his people's naturism: 'The rites of this physical worship, again, were wholly symbolic, and the Indian no more worshiped the Sun than the Christian adores the Cross' (Eastman 1911: 13).[9]

Now, the symbolic interpretation refers us to a basic dichotomy in man's comprehension of reality, a distinction between a natural and a supernatural reality. To avoid misunderstanding, it is here not a question of a distinction in a philosophical sense, between two absolutely separate worlds, but a more practical distinction between an everyday reality and a reality of another order to which spirits and miracles belong (cf. Arbman 1939: 26 f.). Religious man is thus concerned with two levels of experience in his cognitive interpretation of the world: the world is usually unequivocal, but sometimes it appears mystified.

This is certainly the view of the Ojibway Indians, although our source-writers tend to deny it. In actual fact, Hallowell provides us with significant examples. He writes that the Ojibway 'recognize, a priori, potentialities for animation in certain classes of objects under certain circumstances. The Ojibwa do not perceive stones, in general, as animate, any more than we do. . . . [However] it is asserted by informants that stones have been seen to move, that some stones manifest other animate properties . . .' (Hallowell 1960 :25). An Ojibway who with his mere word could induce a bear to withdraw 'was not confronted with an animal with objective ursine properties, but rather with an animate being who had ursine attributes and *also* person attributes' (Hallowell 1960: 36). 'My Ojibwa friends,' Hallowell continues, 'often cautioned me against judging by appearances. A poor forlorn Indian dressed in rags might have great power; a smiling, amiable woman, or a pleasant old man, might be a sorceror. . . . What looks like an animal, without great power, may be a transformed person with evil intent' (Hallowell 1960: 39 f.; cf. also Jenness 1935: 27).

We might have expected that with these statements Hallowell would have wanted to illustrate a dichotomy between natural and supernatural in Ojibway thought, but this is far from the case. On the contrary, he assures us that the appellation supernatural, 'if applied to the Ojibwa characters, is completely misleading, if for no other reason than the fact that the concept of supernatural presupposes a concept of the natural. The latter is not present in Ojibwa thought' (Hallowell 1960: 28). Jenness has made pronouncements of a similar kind (Jenness 1935: 29). It is obvious to Hallowell that the Ojibway view of reality is different from ours; the examples he adduces and which have just been quoted demonstrate, in his opinion, that anthropomorphism and metamorphoses are part of the Ojibway manner of conceiving the world around them. This is certainly correct in itself, but at the same time constitutes an insufficient explanation. The interesting fact is that the models of cognition change, that there is a span between the interpretations in different situations.

This is why the distinction between natural and supernatural falls into place. This distinction need in no way be as philosophically refined as Hallowell has in mind: it is simply there, a matter of religious conviction. Nor need this distinction be a conscious one so that the natural, or the supernatural, makes up a linguistic category of its own (which, nevertheless, is the case among some North American tribes). As Dorothy Lee says concerning the Californian Wintu Indians, 'natural necessity is beyond question, and demands no proof. It is only implied; there is no name for it. The supernatural is named and can be spoken of' (Lee 1975: 140). Also the Ojibway know the term for the supernatural: it is *manitou* (Jones 1905). For the rest, the correspondence between conscious and linguistic categories is not always there. As Hallowell himself emphasizes, the Ojibway are not conscious of the distinction between 'animate' and 'inanimate', although it is implied in their language (Hallowell 1960: 23).

It is thus obvious that the Ojibway like other religious peoples have de facto proceeded from a dichotomy between natural and supernatural. This dichotomy was largely unreflected (it is tempting to call it an 'etic' category, but it is more than that). Thus, it did not lead to the consequence of a logically accomplished bisection of reality. The masters of the animals belong in principle to the supernatural world, but, as we have seen, they may be both killed and eaten.

180

We may now draw the conclusions of this study. If there is this dichotomy between natural and supernatural, and if religion means a symbolic interpretation of the supernatural reality, then it is impossible to deduce religion from experiences of nature. Instead, the streaks of nature features in a certain religion should be understood as descriptive symbols of the different reality, hard to understand, that is the supernatural reality. The stronger the connection between man and his natural environment is, the more obvious is the transference of nature symbolism to the figures of the supernatural world. Ojibway religion has a definite concentration on the hunting situation, and therefore the spirits and rituals of hunting play such a dominant role.

Seen in this perspective the elements of nature are only the garments, the symbols, which the divine (or the supernatural) breaks through. Religious intuition is primary, the fixation of religion at natural objects is secondary.

Notes

1 An earlier attempt at measuring the impact of nature on North American religions was made by Konrad Theodor Preuss (1905), a study in the spirit of environmental determinism.

2 The western high plains were the home-grounds of the mounted Plains Indian hunters, the eastern prairies the domains of Indians who were both hunters and maize cultivators. On the difference between Plains and Prairie Indians, see Kroeber 1939: 76 ff., Hartmann 1973: 7 f., Hultkrantz 1973: 4 f.

3 This idea was however never carried as far as a modern anthropologist imagines when he reports that the young Beaver Indians (in northern Alberta) during their puberty vision quest 'do live with animals and learn to speak their language' (Ridington 1971: 122).

4 I cannot endorse Werner Müller's opinion that the idea of an hostile environment is not American Indian, but a learned cliché (Müller 1976: 42). Even the hunters may under certain conditions apprehend nature as evil, cf. below.

5 The late origin of the family hunting grounds as a consequence of the fur trade was pointed out by Eleanor Leacock (1954). For a review of the discussion in this matter, see Martin 1975: 117 ff.

6 The occurrence of clans in earlier social structure among the Ojibway is still an open question; objections have been raised by E. S. Rogers and J. G. E. Smith. However, it appears probable to me that the Ojibway once assimilated the clan organization existing among the Central Algonkians south of the Great Lakes, with whom they also shared certain religious customs and rituals (cf. below). The connection with the Central Algonkian clan organization has been stressed by Bishop (1976: 50 ff.). See also Callender 1962, Dräger 1968.

7 According to Hickerson, the settlements in big villages were the social and economic prerequisites of the presence of both 'the feast of the dead' – a ceremony with secondary burial of the bones of the earlier deceased in ossuaries and trans-

mission of their glorious names to new generations – and 'the great medicine ceremony' or *midewiwin* – a ritual complex at which men who had received instruction for the purpose were initiated into the shamanic *mide* society, composed of members who, by the aid of white sea shells (*megis*) and medicine bags, were thought to be able to kill as well as cure. Hickerson thinks that the feast of the dead had its origins in the Algonkian and Iroquoian prehistoric past in the Eastern Woodlands. The *midewiwin,* on the other hand, he considers to be a late product, the result of the acculturation in the country south of Lake Superior during the eighteenth century (Hickerson 1960, 1962 a, 1963). I share Hickerson's opinion about the remote origins of the feast of the dead – it appears to me that it might be referred back to the burial cults of Hopewell times about two thousand years ago. On the other hand, Hickerson's proofs of a recent origin of the *midewiwin* are not convincing. It may be argued that in its present form, as a secret medicine society, it is fairly recent, but, as Werner Müller has shown, it contains vestiges of an old new year's rite. We know, for instance, that the *megis* symbolized tribal unity and that according to old sources the ceremony created 'yearly a national gathering' (Hickerson 1970: 56, 58). I would offer the hypothesis that, under the influences from the mescal cult flourishing along the Mississippi River, a transformation took place of an original annual rite to a secret society.

8 In the aftermath of epidemics followed tularemia and other diseases from the Old World that wiped out the animal population, thus negatively influencing hunting luck and hunting beliefs (Martin 1978: 130 ff.).

9 The tendency to conceive environment in symbolic forms was well developed among these Dakota, see also Fire and Erdoes 1972 :108 ff.

Bibliography

Arbman, E.
  1939 Mythic and Religious Thought. Pp. 20–40 in Dragma, M. P. Nilsson Dedicatum. Lund.
Bishop, Ch. A.
  1976 The Emergence of the Northern Ojibwa: Social and Economic Consequences. American Ethnologist 3 (1): 39–54.
Brown, J. E.
  1953 The Sacred Pipe. Norman, Oklahoma.
Callender, Ch.
  1962 Social Organization of the Central Algonkian Indians. Milwaukee Public Museum, Publications in Anthropology No. 7. Milwaukee.
Cooper, J .M.
  1933 The Northern Algonquian Supreme Being. Primitive Man 6 (3–4): 41–111.
  1936 Notes on the Ethnology of the Otchipwe of Lake of the Woods and Rainy Lake. The Catholic University of America, Anthropological Series No. 3. Washington.
  1939 Is the Algonquian Family Hunting Ground System Pre-Columbian? American Anthropologist 41 (1): 66–90.
Copway, G.
  1850 The Traditional History and Characteristic Sketches of the Ojibway Nation. London.
  1851 Recollections of A Forest Life. London.
Dobyns, H. F.
  1976 Native American Historical Demography. Bloomington.

Dorsey, G. A.
  1905 The Cheyenne, I. Ceremonial Organization. Field Columbian Museum, Anthropological Series 9 (1). Chicago.
Dräger, L.
  1968 Formen der lokalen Organisation bei den Stämmen der Zentral-Algonkin von der Zeit ihrer Entdeckung bis zur Gegenwart. Berlin.
Driver, H. E.
  1961 Indians of North America. Chicago.
Dunning, R. W.
  1959 Social and Economic Change among the Northern Ojibwa. Toronto.
Eastman, Ch. A.
  1911 The Soul of the Indian. Boston and New York.
Erikson, K. T. and Ch. Vecsey
  1980 A Report to the People of Grassy Narrows. Pp. 152–161 in American Indian Environments, ed. by Ch. Vecsey and R. W. Venables. Syracuse, New York.
Feit, H. A.
  1973 Twilight of the Cree Hunting Nation. Natural History, August–September 1973.
Fire, J. and R. Erdoes
  1972 Lame Deer: Seeker of Visions. New York.
Flannery, R.
  1940 The Cultural Position of the Spanish River Indians. Primitive Man 13 (1–2): 1–25.
Hallowell, A. I.
  1926 Bear Ceremonialism in the Northern Hemisphere. American Anthropologist 28 (1): 1–175.
  1934 Some Empirical Aspects of Northern Saulteaux Religion. American Anthropologist 36 (3): 389–404.
  1942 The Role of Conjuring in Saulteaux Society. Publications of the Philadelphia Anthropological Society, Vol. 2. Philadelphia.
  1955 Culture and Experience. Philadelphia.
  1960 Ojibwa Ontology, Behavior, and World View. Pp. 19–52 in Culture in History, ed. by S. Diamond. New York.
Hartmann, H.
  1973 Die Plains- und Prairieindianer Nordamerikas. Berlin.
Hickerson, H.
  1960 The Feast of the Dead among the Seventeenth Century Algonkians of the Upper Great Lakes. American Anthropologist 62 (1): 81–107.
  1962 a Notes on the Post-Contact Origin of the Midewiwin. Ethnohistory 9 (4): 404–423.
  1962 b The Southwestern Chippewa: An Ethnohistorical Study. Memoirs of the American Anthropological Association No. 92. Menasha.
  1963 The Sociohistorical Significance of Two Chippewa Ceremonials. American Anthropologist 65 (1): 67–85.
  1967 Some Implications of the Theory of the Particularity, or 'Atomism', of Northern Algonkians. Current Anthropology 8 (4): 313–343.
  1970 The Chippewa and Their Neighbors: A Study in Ethnohistory. New York.
Hultkrantz, Å.
  1953 Conceptions of the Soul among North American Indians. Statens etnografiska museum, Monograph Series No. 1. Stockholm.
  1954 The Indians and the Wonders of Yellowstone: A Study of the Interrelations of Religion, Nature and Culture. Ethnos 19: 34–68.

1961 The Owner of the Animals in the Religion of the North American Indians. Pp. 53–64 in Stockholm Studies in Comparative Religion No. 1. Stockholm.
1968 La divination en Amérique du Nord. Pp. 69–149 in La divination, ed. by A. Caquot and M. Leibovici ,Vol. II. Paris.
1972 The Elusive Totemism. Pp. 218–227 in Studies in the History of Religions Vol. 22. Leiden.
1973 Prairie and Plains Indians. Iconography of Religions, Vol. 10 (3). Leiden.
1978 The Cult of the Dead among North American Indians. Temenos 14: 97–126.
1979 a Ecology of Religion: Its Scope and Methodology. Pp. 221–236 in Science of Religion: Studies in Methodology, ed. by L. Honko. The Hague.
1979 b Naturkänsla, ekologi och religion i indianernas Nordamerika. Pp. 109–117 in Acta Societatis Anthropologicae Fennicae No. 5. Helsinki.
1979 c The Fear of Geysers among Indians of the Yellowstone Park Area. Pp. 33–42 in Lifeways of Intermontane and Plains Montana Indians, ed. by L. B. Davis. Museum of the Rockies Occasional Papers No. 1. Bozeman, Montana.
1979 d The Religions of the American Indians. Berkeley, Los Angeles, London.
1980 a The Development of the Plains Indian Sun Dance. Pp. 225–243 in Perennitas, ed. by G. Piccaluga . Rome.
1980 b The Problem of Christian Influence on Northern Algonkian Eschatology. Studies in Religion 9 (2): 161–183.
1981 Belief and Worship in Native North America. Syracuse, New York.
Ms Three Views on the Function of Religious Symbols, lecture held at conference on methods in religion, Warsaw, September 1979 (in press).
Jenness, D.
1935 The Ojibwa Indians of Parry Island: Their Social and Religious Life. National Museum of Canada, Bulletin No. 78. Ottawa.
Jones, W.
1905 The Algonkin Manitou. Journal of American Folklore 18: 183–190.
Karsten, R.
1935 The Origins of Religion. London.
Kock, G.
1956 Der Heilbringer. Ein Beitrag zur Aufklärung seiner religionsgeschichtlichen Voraussetzungen. Ethnos 21 (1–2): 118–129.
Kohl, J. G.
1859 Kitschi-Gami oder Erzählungen vom Obern See. 2 volumes. Bremen.
Krech, S. III
1978 Disease, Starvation, and Northern Athapaskan Social Organization. American Ethnologist 5 (4): 710–732.
Kroeber, A. L.
1939 Cultural and Natural Areas of Native North America. Berkeley.
Lahontan, Baron de
1905 New Voyages to North-America, ed. by R. G. Thwaites. 2 volumes. Chicago.
Landes, R.
1937 Ojibwa Sociology. Columbia University Contributions to Anthropology, Vol. 29. New York.
Leacock, E.
1954 The Montagnais 'Hunting Territory' and the Fur Trade. Memoirs of the American Anthropological Association No. 78. Menasha.
Lee, D.
1975 Linguistic Reflection of Wintu Thought. Pp. 130–140 in Teachings from

the American Earth: Indian Religion and Philosophy, ed. by D. Tedlock and
B. Tedlock. New York.

Long, J.
1791 Voyages and Travels of an Indian Interpreter and Trader. London.

Lubbock, J.
1870 The Origin of Civilisation and the Primitive Condition of Man. London.

Marett, R. R.
1909 The Threshold of Religion. London.

Martin, C.
1975 The Four Lives of a Micmac Copper Pot. Ethnohistory 22 (2): 111–133.
1978 Keepers of the Game: Indian-Animal Relationships and the Fur Trade. Berkeley, Los Angeles, London.

Müller, W.
1972 Geliebte Erde: Naturfrömmigkeit und Naturhass im indianischen und euro-
päischen Nordamerika. Bonn.
1976 Indianische Welterfahrung. Stuttgart.

Paproth, H.-J. R.
1976 Studien über das Bärenzeremoniell, I. Bärenjagdriten und Bärenfeste bei den
tungusischen Völkern. Uppsala.

Parker, S.
1960 The Wiitiko Psychosis in the Context of Ojibwa Personality and Culture.
American Anthropologist 62 (4): 603–623.

Paulson, I.
1959 Zur Aufbewahrung der Tierknochen im nördlichen Nordamerika. Pp. 182–
188 in Mitteilungen aus dem Museum für Völkerkunde in Hamburg, Vol.
25. Hamburg.
1961 Schutzgeister und Gottheiten des Wildes (der Jagdtiere und Fische) in Nord-
eurasien. Stockholm Studies in Comparative Religion No. 2 . Stockholm.
1964 The Animal Guardian. History of Religions 3 (2): 202–219.
1965 Die rituelle Erhebung des Bärenschädels bei arktischen und subarktischen
Völkern. Temenos 1: 150–173.

Pettazzoni, R.
1954 Essays on the History of Religions. Leiden.

Preuss, K. Th.
1905 Der Einfluss der Natur auf die Religion in Mexiko und den Vereinigten
Staaten. Zeitschrift der Gesellschaft für Erdkunde zu Berlin: 361–408.

Radin, P.
1936 Ojibwa and Ottawa Puberty Dreams. Pp. 233–264 in Essays in Anthropology, ed. by R. H. Lowie. Berkeley.

Ridington, R.
1971 Beaver Indian Dreaming and Singing. Anthropologica 13 (1–2): 115–128.

Skinner, A.
1911 Notes on the Eastern Cree and Northern Saulteaux. Anthropological Papers
of the American Museum of Natural History, Vol. 9 (1). New York.

Speck, F. G.
1915 The Family Hunting Band as the Basis of Algonkian Social Organization.
American Anthropologist 17 (3): 289–305.

Speck, F. G. and G. G. Heye
1921 Hunting Charms of the Montagnais and the Mistassini. Indian Notes and
Monographs. New York.

Steward, J. H.
1955 Theory of Culture Change. Urbana, Illinois.

185

Tanner, A.
  1979 Bringing Home Animals: Religious Ideology and Mode of Production of the Mistassini Cree Hunters. New York.
Teicher, M. I.
  1960 Windigo Psychosis: A Study of a Relationship between Belief and Behavior among the Indians of Northeastern Canada. Proceedings of the American Ethnological Society. Seattle and London.
Thompson, S.
  1929 Tales of the North American Indians. Cambridge, Mass.
Trigger, B. G. (ed.)
  1978 Handbook of North American Indians, Vol. 15: Northeast. Washington.
Turner, H.
  1976 The Earthly and the Heavenly: The Interactions of Geography and Religions. Mimeographed copy, University of Otago, New Zealand.
Tylor, E. B.
  1891 Primitive Culture. 2 volumes. Third edition, London.
Vecsey, Ch.
  1980 American Indian Environmental Religions. Pp. 1–37 in American Indian Environments, ed. by Ch. Vecsey and R. W. Venables. Syracuse, New York.
  Ms Traditional Ojibwa Religion and Its Historical Changes (in press).
Weule, K.
  1921 Die Kultur der Kulturlosen. Stuttgart.
Wissler, C.
  1950 The American Indian. Third edition, New York.
Witthoft, J.
  1949 Green Corn Ceremonialism in the Eastern Woodlands. Occasional Contributions from the Museum of Anthropology of the University of Michigan Vol. 13. Ann Arbor.

The Hunter and the Animal in Present-Day Folk-Tales in Iceland

Haraldur Olafsson

Anyone who has grown up on a farm knows what strong feelings one develops there for animals and their behaviour. The animals have their given role in all that takes place there. Human beings, animals and all living creatures form an entirety, a closed homogenic world, where people and animals are of the same nature. This is a well-known phenomenon all over the world. Among so-called 'primitive' people the animal plays an important role, and the people and animals are often related to each other.

In this paper some conceptions concerning hunting in Iceland will be examined. However, one should not expect a strong feeling for hunting, since Iceland has been a typical farming community for many decades. But besides farming the farmers have carried out a considerable amount of hunting. Fishing has always been important for the household economy, and during the later middle ages fish was an important export product. It is noticeable how much survives today of the belief and superstition attached to fishing amongst the fishing population.

Circumstances concerning the catch and the hunted animals will not be dealt with here, but instead some features will be presented concerning belief and attitude towards a species of animal that has a special position among mammals in Iceland, namely the fox.

From my childhood I have heard a considerable number of tales and stories about the braininess and genial cunningness of the fox. When it comes to slyness only the raven can be compared with the fox.

The fox maintains a special position amongst the animals in Iceland. It is the only land mammal that is indigenous to Iceland (polar bears have only appeared there sporadically). The fox has never been important as edible food in the country. One cannot eat fox-meat, and fox fur has never been especially sought after. At certain times though it has been of value as an export article. The fox often caused serious damage by killing lambs in the springtime and even old sheep. It also drives away birds from their nests, eats their eggs and their young. The collecting of eggs from sea-birds was rather important in some areas of the country, and particular care was therefore taken to chase the fox away from nesting cliffs. Already in the old laws of Iceland there are stipulations concerning fox-hunting and the banning of sending 'wolf', that is fox, to the country (Grágás II, 1879: 373). The tradition of fox-hunting is very ancient in Iceland, and in connection with this a certain view has developed concerning the behaviouristics of fox-hunting, a view that is reflected in stories and adventures (Thoroddsen 1911: 445).

The purpose of this paper is not to find a pattern in animal fables or tales, but to investigate the attitude of the hunter towards the animals he hunts and how hunting methods and the hunting philosophy influence each other. Fox-hunting has a function other than the catch itself. This is only indirectly a stage in the provision of food. Instead it resembles entertainment rather than a necessary pursuit. Fox-hunting is almost a sport, which is useful to the farming community.

The present author grew up on a farm. The farm was situated close to a lava field where there was an abundance of foxes. Every year in the early summer the men went out into the fields and up in the mountains to hunt fox. This was done during May to June when the female fox had given birth to her young. In connection with this activity one heard a number of stories about the intelligence and logical way of thinking of the fox. One heard that man and animal must learn from each other, and one could not catch a fox without knowing much about its life, intelligence and the way it thought.

These fox-hunters worked for the community. They were often very good ptarmigan hunters during the winters. (Ptarmigan-hunting has none of the mystery and belief conceptions associated with fox-hunting.)

In order to investigate the connection between the hunter and the animal I have perused some tales by such professional hunters. Some of the most interesting ones are in a book by Theódór Gunnlaugsson, a farmer in the north of Iceland. He still writes about hunting and nature conservation in the daily papers. In the book Á refaslóðum (1955) he describes the methods of hunting which he thinks are the most rewarding. There are also a number of tales about the fox and his experiences of foxes. He philosophizes about animals and humans, and provides engaging descriptions of the behaviour of animals.

In two books (1973 and 1974) Thórdur Halldorssôn has described his experience of fox-hunting. Gudmundur Einarsson (1960) has given fine accounts of fox-hunting during a long life. Tryggvi Einarsson (1978) has great experience of all types of hunting, and Jón Gudmundsson (1922) has written a 'textbook' on fox-hunting. All these accounts are of great value.

What do these experienced hunters tell us about the behaviour of animals, their thoughts and knowledge? How do they regard the relations between humans and animals? What do they think the world looks like from the animals' viewpoint? All this touches on a very important and complicated question, that is: what is the 'world-view of these hunters'?

In Theódór Gunnlaugsson's tales there are comprehensive stories concerning most aspects of fox-hunting. Every species of animal has its own distinctive characteristics, which differentiate it from other species. Individuals within each species are different and have their own personalities, wills, and knowledge. One really doesn't find such a great difference between humans and animals. Humans, are however, superior to animals in most aspects. The similarities are that animals reason, plan, and learn from experience, just like humans. Concisely one could say that the conclusions of Gunnlaugsson and the other fox-hunters are as follows: the hunt is a battle between two intelligent beings, where the man only has the upper hand if he has very good knowledge of the nature and behaviour pattern of the animal and its way of reasoning.

Gunnlaugsson writes: 'I soon discovered that some (foxes) made use of a cunning, which I knew without a doubt, could only exist in a human brain, a very intelligent brain to boot' (1955: 9) ('Fann ég þá brátt, ad sumir þeirra beittu brögum, sem mér kom ekki til hugar ad gætu átt upptök sín annars stadar en í mannsheila, og þad óvenju snjöllum mannsheila'). And as a logical concequence the conclusion was that to succeed in hunting one must find the right counter-move to the next move of the animal. The animal reasons and makes plans according to the same pattern as a human. The hunt is a battle between equals, but the human can learn those tricks which serve to give him the upper hand.

Gunnlaugsson gives a comprehensive description of the two species of fox that exist in Iceland, that is the polar fox and the red-brown fox, and he compares their intelligence. The polar fox is of the same species as the Greenland fox and the white-fox in the arctic islands north of Canada and Svalbard. Without a doubt they have come over to Iceland on the ice, probably already in the ice-age, but possibly later on with the pack-ice from Greenland (Saemundsson 1923). According to the opinions of the Iceland fox-hunters, the polar fox has been easy for the hunters to catch, but over decades it has increased its knowledge and learnt from experience. This is quite in line with the ethologists' view of animal behaviour (compare also Darwin: 'In North-America where the fur-bearing animals have long been pursued, they exhibit, according to the unanimous testimony of all observers, an almost incredible amount of sagacity, caution and cunning, but trapping has been there so long carried on, that inheritance may possibly have come into play' (1906: 121–122)).

The red-brown fox must have come from Europe, and probably from Norway. It is almost out of the question that the red-brown fox came to Iceland over land. It has come by boat. Why it should have been transported over the sea is unknown. There is a tale that Saamis who wanted revenge on the Icelandic People sent it over (Huld 1922), and other tales tell that a Norwegian woman sent the fox to Iceland as a revenge for her son who had been murdered in Iceland. The law in Grágás prohibiting the sending of wolves to Iceland might have come about because someone took the fox to Iceland in order to have enough fox pelts in the country. In any case the red-brown fox is 'European', which means that it has a long and ingrown experience of the human being. Theódór says that it is a quick-thinker, discovers danger quicker than the polar fox, and is cunning when it comes to finding a way out of a difficult situation. All this depends on its experience of human beings. (It is remarkable that, in an article by one of the best-known fox-hunters during later times, not a word is said about the intelligence of the fox or the difference between the two species (Johann Halldórsson 1900)).

Gunnlaugsson's ethological observations are highly relevant to the understanding of his conclusions. They are constantly concerned with natural science, a natural science which firstly and lastly is founded on a deep understanding of the connection between all units of an ecological system, and the behaviour of the animal. When one sets out a trap, or waits at the burrows, or puts out poison in nature, one must carry out these things with the behaviour of the animal in mind. But since humans and animals think in the same way and know each other's thoughts and habits, they are evenly matched (Gunnlaugsson 1955: 84 f.). The animal can therefore take the initiative and decide the development of events and therefore force the hunter to keep changing his plans.

The human being has however a positive factor in his favour: it is he who decides to go out and seek the fox. The fox never has this initiative – it is always the one to be hunted. What can happen is that the fox can have a forewarning of the human without the hunter noticing. The Iceland hunters then think that in this type of case it is almost impossible to catch the animal, since it is so forewarned and flees from all contact with the man, and simply diseappears. If the human sees the animal without being noticed by it, then the hunter has every possibility of catching it. But it very often happens that the animal sees the hunter after a while and then begins a battle of positions, cunning and slyness which characterizes fox-hunting. In the other stories that have been investigated one meets exactly the same line of thought as in Theódór Gunnlaugsson. All these descriptions are based on experience and events, and the author tries to find 'natural' explanations for the behaviour of the animal. Gunnlaugsson's method is scientific, more precisely: ethologic. He sees patterns in the behaviour of animals, and this pattern shows the animal's capacity to think and draw conclusions. According to Gunnlaugsson's ideas, the animal is a being capable of thought, not only guided by instincts but to a high degree by intelligence. He would not accept all the ethologists' views on this problem, for instance not Koehler's dictum: 'There is an innate capacity for communication in all members of species, together with comprehension of the significance of the releaser mechanism. This innate comprehension has nothing to do with intelligence. All features are self-evident and have nothing to do with achievement' (Koehler 1972: 84). Lorenz's theory concerning intelligence as collected experiences in the mind is more in line with Gunnlaugsson's thoughts (Lorenz 1977: 65 and 128).

Gunnlaugsson is very familiar with the position of the fox in the ecological system. He knows what it lives off, under which circumstances it eats lamb or egg or poultry. He knows the way in which it chooses places in which to mate, and where to have its lair. He describes differences between animals in different parts of the country, and he thinks that he can discern differences in the nature of the fox, and how varying ecological conditions create varying patterns of behaviour. In all this he is on the same line as the scientists. But he goes on further and mixes all this natural science together with animal psychology. For him it isn't enough to explain behaviouristic patterns from surroundings, instincts, and learnt responses. This cannot explain everything. Only if one reckons with the animal possessing intelligence and being capable of logical thought, an abstract form of thought, can one explain its responses and behaviour. Certainly, animals learn much from experience, but knowledge that has been learnt cannot explain its behaviour in new and previously unknown situations.

This mixture of natural science and philosphical reflections is rather common among the fox-hunters who write about their experiences. But also, among those who have written about pets, one finds similar attitudes. An Icelandic farmer has, in some books, described horses and sheep, especially those individuals among the sheep called *leader* sheep (*forystufé*), and horses that have been known to be clever and unusually good riding horses (Jónsson 1946, 1948 and 1953). Jónsson gives exhaustive studies of rational and logical behaviour among animals, and their capacity to meet new situations in an intelligent way.

Theódór Gunnlaugsson mentions many examples of how both young and adult foxes are more on their guard in areas where fox-hunting has been going on for a long time than in other areas where they have been living undisturbed. Jón Gudmundsson describes how the poisoning of foxes has failed after a while because the fox has learnt how dangerous it is to take poisoned food (1922: 86 f.). Also Thordur Halldórsson tells how adult foxes stop young ones from eating poisoned food (1973: 137). All this is natural science, and in accord with observations from other parts of the world. Darwin quotes Leroy like this, to mention an example: 'Leroy states that in districts where foxes are much hunted, the young, on first leaving their burrows, are incontestably, much more wary than the old ones in districts where they are not much hunted' (Darwin 1906: 122).

The really interesting thing is that, in the fox-hunter's interpretation and attitude towards the animal, one can see a glimpse of an ancient attitude towards the animal world – to the hunter's world. There we have 'a world-view', where all living things are of the same nature, they obey the same laws of nature, and all belong to one family. Humans and animals form a unit in nature, humans become animals and animals become humans. This 'primitive' viewpoint asserts itself very clearly in almost everything that has been written about fox-hunting.

One may then question whether or not this attitude can be associated with religious conceptions of so-called primitive people? Is there anything in this attitude that can be put in connection with magical conceptions or ritual?

One has not been able to find any form of ritual concerning fox-hunting. Probably every hunter has a form of supernatural belief, and possibly he follows certain individual rules in the hunt and in the preparations before the hunt. But there is no mention.of this in the sources on which this paper is based. One does not know whether there are any special general rules of taboo connected with hunting. There is nothing said about individual rules of taboo. Characteristics attributed to hunters nowadays are firstly and lastly those that deal with attitudes towards nature. Nature has something living over it, and humans and animals belong to the same nature. Hultkrantz expresses it thus: 'In the development of the belief in souls among animals, plants and objects we find a pure expression of the fellow-feeling of the primitive hunter and collector with nature' (1953: 497).

Knud Rasmussen mentions many examples from the Eskimoes concerning the close connection between a human being and an animal. An Eskimo says 'We believe . . . that there has been a time when there was not much difference between an animal's soul and a human's soul. All living things were very much alike' (1931: 217). The concept of the soul has a long history in Icelandic folk belief and the Icelandic hunters are treading on well-trod soil (compare Ólafsson 1977).

Much points to the fact that there really isn't much difference between primitive and 'civilized' people when it comes to their attitude towards nature. Frazer expresses this well: 'The explanation of life by the theory of an indwelling and practically immortal soul is one which the savage does not confine to human beings but extends to the animal creation in general . . . (The savage) . . . commonly believes that animals are endowed with feelings and intelligence like those of men, and that, like man, they possess souls which survive the death of their bodies either to wander about as disembodied spirits or to be born again in animal form' (1936: 204). Everything in this quotation could be taken directly from the fox-hunters' philosophy, and even from many farmers' attitude towards cattle. Because one can count on humans and animals possessing the same qualities of soul, one can be sure of the animals' reaction and behaviour in certain situations. Knowledge of the ethology of animals is not enough – one must always count on an intelligence much the same as a human's intelligence. Darwin has expressed this very well when he writes: 'It is significant fact that the more the habits of any particular animal are studied by a naturalist, the more he attributes to reason and less to inherent instincts' (1906: 114). It is precisely this that is so interesting in the fox-hunter's interpretation of the behaviour of animals. Their observation is accurate, but they consider that the behaviour cannot be explained as having come from conditioned reflexes, learnt habits, or traumatic experiences (compare Lorenz 1977: 77 f). This does not suffice to explain the responses of the animals. In addition there must be a logical way of thinking, which on all counts is like a human being's way of reasoning. This attitude is 'primitive' and part of the world view where everything is alive, with soul, and obeying the same laws of nature, and is one and the same family. The history of man can be divided into two periods: first of all man was a mammal amongst others, living in peace in nature without fear of being in danger. When man started to hunt other animals the balance of the whole way of life changed. The animal started to fear man more than any other animal species (compare Washburn and Lancaster 1968: 299). There is a connection between the hunter and the animal that has its roots in the prehistoric semi-darkness, a connection, based on knowledge of nature and life, which very rarely prevails among others than those who live in close contact with nature. To succeed in the hunt depends on two important factors: firstly the hunter must be familiar with animal ethology, and secondly, no less important, he must have good luck in the hunt (compare Ólafsson 1978 and Laughlin 1968: 308). It would be stretching a point to discuss luck in hunting, but there is every reason to believe that it depends on, at least to a small degree, the hunter's ability to influence the development of events through some kind of spiritual contact with the animal (Gudmundur Einarsson 1960: 142). This belief, that man and animal are of the same family and that both have a similar soul, gives rise to such a contact. This also causes one to count on similar characteristics in other areas, for example, a logical, abstract way of thought and reasoning which is based on collective experience of the species.

From those stories which this investigation is based upon concerning the Icelandic fox-hunters' attitude towards the fox, one can discern some main points.

1) The relationship man: animal is characterized thus that both are of the same nature, obey the same psychological laws, think in a similar way and reason likewise.
2) The animal has the same feeling of emotion as man, plus two: a feeling of predominant danger, and an ability to orientate (all the authors mention this almost supernatural ability to find the right way).
3) The animal owns a 'soul' as does man.
4) The hunt is a battle between equals, where he who has the initiative has the advantage.

The Icelandic fox-hunters base their interpretation of the fox's capabilities on direct and lengthy observation. This has nothing to do with belief and superstition. They draw their conclusions from that they have seen and experienced. Their method is ecological and ethological. All that they have experienced in connection with the behaviour and responses of the fox in given situations points to a thinking capacity in the fox, a

194

thinking capacity that works in the same way as that of a human. Through this lengthy observation they arrive at the aforementioned conclusions. In my opinion one can find here a direct connection with the world view of 'primitive' hunters, which is also founded on direct experience and observation.

One cannot say that the investigations made by the Icelandic foxhunters are founded on experiments according to scientific rules. Their conclusions are possibly wrong and their explanations vague and unscientific. But they have one thing in common with hunters throughout time: they succeed in the hunt because their knowledge is so great. Their conclusions and explanations lead to a good result in the hunt. And to succeed the hunter has, for a while, to be one with the animal, be the animal, and therefore have the same qualities as the animal, and the animal will be one with the man.

Bibliography

Darwin, Ch.
    1906 The Descent of Man and Selection in Relation to Sex. London.
Einarsson, G.
    1960 Nú brosir nóttin. Reykjavik.
Einarsson, T.
    1978 Í veidihug. Reykjavik.
Frazer, J. G.
    1936 The Golden Bough, Vol. II. London.
Friedrich, H. (ed.)
    1972 Man and Animal. London.
Grágás II
    1879 Copenhagen.
Gudmundsson, J.
    1922 Melrakkar nútímans. Búnadarrit 36 (4). Reykjavik.
Gunnlaugsson, Th.
    1955 Á refaslódum. Reykjavik.
Halldórsson, J.
    1900 Um refaveidar, Andvari. Reykjavik.
Halldórsson, Th.
    1973 Mannleg náttúra undir jökli. Reykjavik.
    1974 Náttúran er söm vid sig. Reykjavik.
Huld, II
    1922 Reykjavik.
Hultkrantz, Å.
    1953 Conceptions of the Soul among North American Indians. Stockholm.
Jónsson, Á.
    1946 Horfnir gódhestar I. Reykjavik.
    1948 Horfnir gódhestar II. Reykjavik.
    1955 Forystufé. Reykjavik.

Koehler, O.
   1972 Prototype of Human Communication Systems in Animals (in: Friedrich 1972). London.
Laughlin, W. S.
   1968 Hunting: An Integrating Biobehavior System and Its Evolutionary Importance. Pp. 304–320 in R. B. Lee and I. DeVore (eds.), Man the Hunter. Chicago.
Lorenz, K.
   1977 Behind the Mirror. New York.
Ólafsson, H.
   1977 Tvaer ritgerdir: Sálnahyggja, trú, töfrar, galdur. Reykjavik.
   1978 Tabus and Hunting Rules among the Central Eskimos, Vol. I. Reykjavik.
Rasmussen, K.
   1931 The Netsilik Eskimos: Social Life and Spiritual Culture. Reports of the Fifth Thule Expedition, Vol. 8 (1). Copenhagen.
Saemundsson, B.
   1923 Spendýrin. Reykjavik.
Thoroddsen, Th.
   1911 Lýsing Íslands, Vol. II. Copenhagen.
Washburn, S. L. and C. S. Lancaster
   1968 The Evolution of Hunting. Pp. 293–303 in R. B. Lee and I. DeVore (eds.), Man the Hunter. Chicago.